The Wedding Dress

How to make the perfect one for you

Becky Drinan

First published 2014 by
GUILD OF MASTER CRAFTSMAN PUBLICATIONS LTD
Castle Place, 166 High Street, Lewes, East Sussex, BN7 1XU

ISBN 978-1-86108-910-6

Publisher **JONATHAN BAILEY**
Production Manager **JIM BULLEY**
Managing Editor **GERRIE PURCELL**
Senior Project Editor **DOMINIQUE PAGE**
Editor **ROBIN PRIDY**
Managing Art Editor **GILDA PACITTI**
Designer **ALI WALPER**
Photographers **CHRIS GLOAG AND BECKY DRINAN**

Set in **DIN, DIDOT, FRENCH SCRIPT**
Colour origination **GMC REPROGRAPHICS**
Printed and bound in China

Contents

Amélie *page 86*

1
Getting Inspired

2
Getting Started

3
The Bridal Wear

Celeste *page 104*

Florence *page 126*

Introduction

With centuries of fashions and trends from which to draw inspiration for a bridal gown, the modern bride is so spoilt for choice it can make the head spin.

Why make your own dress?

Making your own dress not only allows you to save on your wedding budget – it gives you the opportunity to have full control over the style, fabric, colours and decoration of one of the most important garments you will ever wear, allowing you to create something unique to you.

Why this book?

This book is written for everyone who is passionate and keen to learn about creating a beautiful dress, whether for yourself or another very lucky lady. You may feel daunted about undertaking such a fabulous project, but don't worry, I have used my years of experience as a bespoke bridal dressmaker to come up with the best tips, suggestions and instructions you will need to get you through this most rewarding undertaking.

From the oft-overlooked undergarments to the all-important understanding of how to show off your assets, from how to thread a needle properly to how to apply the most delicate, hand-stitched lace draping – all you need to get the wedding dress of your dreams is in here.

The instructions themselves have also been broken into manageable steps, with lots of pictures to help you along as well as options for variations such as cap sleeves, detachable trains and embellishments. And don't forget, the three dresses in this book are merely a template for your own design. Whether it be the fabrics, cut or decorative touches that inspire you, each one can be tweaked to incorporate your ideas and showcase your personal style.

A present to yourself

Involve your friends and family as much
or as little as you like but also set aside
a space where you can work undisturbed
– preferably somewhere you can store your
dress without it being crammed into a
drawer or accidentally becoming a cat bed...

Most importantly, give yourself the time to
make the dress yours and yours alone, one
made with plenty of love and style, unique
to you. From measuring up and choosing
the fabrics to designing accessories and
fitting the dress, this book gives you the
opportunity to take charge, so go for it!

Let's begin the journey of
creating the most significant
dress of your life...

How to Use this Book

You may already have clear ideas about the style of dress you want, or you may be totally lost in the whirl of bridal choice. You may be an experienced seamstress, or new to dressmaking. Whatever your stage, this book will guide you through every step it takes to make your dream wedding dress.

Be prepared...

This book is to be read for both inspiration and instruction. The beginning chapter, 'Getting Inspired', runs through how to make the most of your figure as well as touches on the key fabrics and little details that will make your dress unique before you start to sketch it out for a final design. Here, we give you a chance to be absolutely certain of your own style, incorporating how your chosen dress will work with the season, the time of day and even the venue.

In 'Getting Started', we lay the groundwork for your actual dress project. Here you will find all the sewing techniques you will need, including what equipment and materials you should have as well as detailed instructions on how to measure yourself properly, how to apply these measurements to the patterns at the back of the book and then make a toile, or mock up of your dress.

Go on, make yourself a dress!

Techniques mastered, measurements taken, patterns and toile done, you are on the way to having the most perfectly fitted dress. At this point, if you haven't done so already, take your time to look through and decide on which of the three dresses you want to

make. Be aware that each dress has certain variations you can choose, be it cap sleeves, a detachable train, draping or applied decorations. Some skirts can be as full or as long as you wish, and all can be worn with or without the additional veil and lace bolero shrug projects provided. You can use the sections on antiquing lace or making a corsage – or not. That is the beauty of designing your dress – the choice is yours!

Each dress project provides step-by-step instructions with images to guide you through drawing your own patterns – be sure to read these through from start to finish before you begin so that you know what fabric, equipment and materials you will need. Tip boxes will provide helpful hints as you go along, and page references are sprinkled throughout the steps, for extra instruction on certain techniques, materials or embellishments.

You may want to get yourself a sewing buddy, ideally someone with sewing or dressmaking knowledge, to help you through this project. At the very least, choose someone with an eye for detail who is good with their hands, and who you are willing to share this personal experience with.

PRACTICE MAKES PERFECT

A substantial section of the book covers sewing techniques that you may need for your dress, from instructions on hems and darts to invisible zips and net underskirts. Designed for you to dip in and out of, you can start practising any unfamiliar techniques until you feel confident, or use the page references dotted throughout the actual dress projects to tackle the technique when required. If you're particularly unsure about a technique, practise first – better to unpick now than on your actual wedding gown.

Getting Inspired

'After all, there is something about a wedding-gown prettier than in any other gown in the world.'

DOUGLAS WILLIAM JERROLD, ENGLISH DRAMATIST

Choosing a Dress Style

Tall and skinny or short and curvy, the proportions of your body are not simply defined by height or weight alone. Identify your assets. Do you have a fabulous bust? Beautiful arms and shoulders? A neat little waist? Shapely legs? Let's make the most of it!

Rather than pigeonhole you into a 'body shape' category, let's look at the parts of your body that you are most pleased with and work out how to make the most of them. Likewise, I'm sure there are bits you'd rather people didn't notice as much, so it's useful to know how to conceal or disguise these as well.

You can do all this and stay true to your personal style. By making your own dress you are not restricted by the bridal shops' idea of what a wedding dress should be. You can play with materials, colours and shapes to create a truly unique dress that is a reflection of your taste.

And while your wedding dress should showcase your personal style, it need not be overpowering. A well-designed dress will show you at your best, so that you look beautiful wearing something that embodies your style and shape, rather than having a dress that is wearing you.

THE PERFECT DRESS FOR YOU
The three dresses made in this book can be adapted to suit all figure types. Working from the basic patterns supplied, you can make a bodice that fits you perfectly, then simply adapt the neck- or waistline and add straps, halters, cap sleeves or even a bolero to suit your shape and look. Hemlines can be raised or lowered and fullness added or taken away from skirts to create the silhouette you desire.

Broad shoulders

Having broad shoulders can make a girl feel at best athletic, at worst masculine.

If you are very slim, dresses probably hang off you like a clothes hanger, but they don't always make you feel feminine or elegant. If you carry more weight it can be very tricky to hide with broad shoulders – the more fabric you add to cover them up, the more bulky they become. But help is at hand!

Choose curved necklines such as a deep scoop or a sweetheart – these will add precious curves to an angular figure. Deep V-necks or scooped necklines will also help to break up a wide upper torso. And with such a broad expanse of chest, you are a perfect backdrop for gorgeous, chunky jewellery – just don't go too tight to the neck. Instead, wear styles that spread out across the chest, towards shoulders and cleavage (**1**).

Avoid straight, harsh horizontal lines – they will only draw attention to your width. Instead, diagonal lines and layering can distract, and opt for soft, drapey or sheer fabrics to add subtle femininity. A halterneck made from wide strips of drapey fabric will look fabulous tied in a floppy bow at the back of the neck (**2**).

A shrug or jacket will soften the outline of muscular or bulky shoulders, and a three-quarter-length sleeve will draw attention down towards the wrists and hands (**3**). Avoid cap sleeves at all costs, as these cut across at the widest point of your silhouette.

Narrow shoulders

Chances are, if you have narrow shoulders then you also have wide hips and a big bottom. We need to redress the balance by adding width to your shoulders, creating an hourglass shape. Avoid strapless dresses or styles with cutaway armholes (unless you are fabulously toned and want to show it off). They will only accentuate your narrowness, making your hips look wider.

Creating more defined shoulders is one of the easiest tricks to achieve. Wearing cap or puffed sleeves (an option for 'Florence', page 154) will add width to your shoulders (**4** & **5**) and, in jackets, always go for a style that fits well but has little shoulder pads to give definition (**6**).

With narrow shoulders, you can get away with wearing shiny and sparkly fabrics. They add volume and attract the eye towards your face, also taking emphasis away from larger areas. Delicate jewellery will look better than anything too chunky, so as not to overpower your small frame.

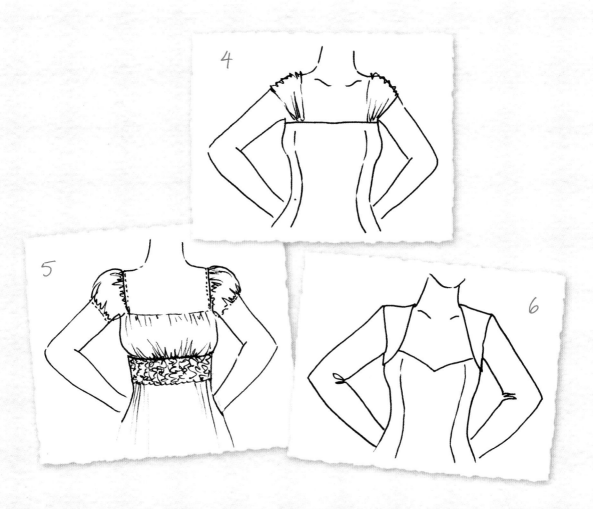

Small bust

You may feel envious of your curvier girlfriends but I bet they envy you when it comes to buying bras. You have more choice – all the multi-way bras and the little lacy numbers are designed for smaller boobs, and you can wear padded, push-up, strapless and even silicone-enhanced styles. To look a bit more voluptuous, get a good padded bra then make sure you are wearing it while taking your measurements.

A straight-across neckline will conceal a lack of natural cleavage and give added width to a narrow chest. You can also carry off detailing over the bust such as ruching, ruffles, frills and sparkle, which would make bustier girls look trussed-up (**7**). Experiment with pretty corsages, lace trims and layered fabrics such as ruched chiffon over shiny satin. You can also use beaded and sequinned fabrics across the bust – these can be expensive, but lucky you, you won't need to buy very much (**8**).

A gently scooping neckline will add the illusion of curves, but don't go too deep or your lack of bust will be clear for the world to see! Or why not look at strapless styles? You don't need hefty bras with shoulder straps, so you can show off a beautiful back and shoulders – just as sexy as a heaving bosom.

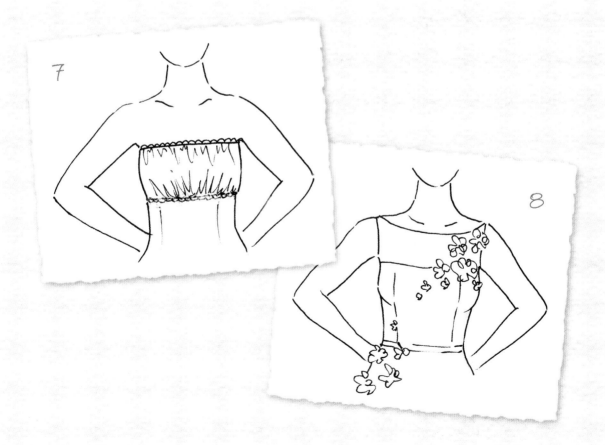

Tiny waist

You are the envy of most women, so make the most of your tiny middle! Corsets were designed to create a figure like yours and will suit your shape perfectly. Going for a boned bodice gives the waist a perfectly smooth silhouette to which you can add all means of decoration to draw attention to this asset. How about a beaded or an elaborate lace fabric at the waist? (**9**) Or you can use a perfectly smooth satin or add a tight sash with a glorious bow to define those curves (**10**).

Small waists can be accentuated further by adding fullness to shoulders, bust and hips – this could be with gentle swathes of chiffon or tulle or with soft crumples of duchesse satin (**11**). Always wear styles that follow the curves of your waist – if you wear a loose style then you'll look as wide as your broadest point, so nip that waist in!

Useful Tip

If you are very slim with no curves but have a tiny waist, make sure to show it off. Pulling in your smallest point will help create a contrast, and make a slim physique look more curvaceous.

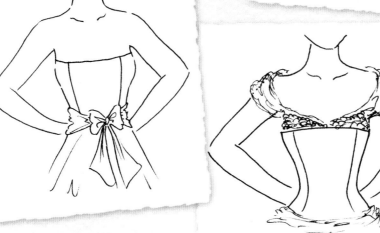

Slim hips

Lucky you! I bet you look great in skinny jeans. You can wear any of the skirt styles in this book but you'll look especially fabulous in the slim, flowing skirt of 'Celeste' (see page 104) (**12**).

Slim hips can carry off shiny fabrics such as crêpe-backed satin – just make sure to wear smooth underwear as it will mercilessly show every contour of what is beneath. To add curves to your hips, go for a nipped-in waist and then add draping or ruching to the hip area, perhaps a corsage or beading to create extra interest (**11**).

Broad hips, big bottom

Circle skirts, princess styles and full hems will all look great on you. Circle skirts flare straight from the waist, skimming over everything from the hips downward (**13**). By using layers and layers of net you can create a really full skirt and no one will know where your real outline is. A-line skirts have less fullness at the hem but still skim over your wobbly bits, creating a beautiful silhouette that can be made more dramatic with a train. Perhaps draw attention to your waist with asymmetrical draping (**14**).

Broad hips can be balanced out by adding width to the shoulders (see also page 16). Avoid shiny/clingy fabrics such as crepe-backed satin, as they will reflect the light and cling to everything, showing off all the lumps and bumps. Instead, opt for crisp fabrics such as taffeta or dupion or soft, drapey fabrics with a matt finish.

Big bust

If you are very busty you'll fall into one of two camps: 'I love my boobs and want to show them off'; or 'I hate my boobs and want to cover them up without drawing attention to their size.'

To disguise an ample bosom, think about a wide-scooped neckline that draws attention to your collarbones, neck and face (**15**). Really pretty jewellery can also draw attention away from your cleavage. Another option is to go for a deep 'V' with a modesty panel – this will break up the expanse of your chest but without showing acres of flesh. It will also direct the eye downwards to a smaller waist (**16**).

Sweetheart necklines look fabulous on you, echoing the wonderful curves of your bust (**17**). By all means, plunge as deep as you dare – but if trying to hide a full bust, better to go for a wide and shallow sweetheart with just a hint of cleavage.

Useful Tip

Make sure to buff and polish your décolletage if it's to be on show, perhaps even adding a little shimmery makeup to highlight your collarbones.

To make the most of this style, you must have a well-fitted bra that gives you lift and a good shape whilst keeping you well held in... we don't want those puppies escaping into the soup at the wedding breakfast!

Bigger boobs can dominate a small frame, so if this is you, make sure your dress pulls in at your narrowest point to create definition between bust, waist and hips. This could make the difference between looking gloriously curvy or just plain lumpy.

Thick waist

You may have a boyish figure with little or no waist definition, or be both busty and broad on the hips but with a belly to match. Either way, diagonal lines are your best friend.

Go for draping and ruching that draws the eye across the body rather than drawing attention to your lack of waist. Asymmetric designs will work well for you, as will careful use of fabrics (**18**).

Satin will bounce the light and can make you look bigger, so think about using this at bust and shoulders, and then from hips to hem. Textured, matt fabrics will absorb light and make an area look smaller, so use this at the waist to create those precious curves (**19**). Adding width or definition to shoulders with cap sleeves or small shoulder pads in a jacket will also help to create a curvier silhouette (**19** & **20**).

Chunky arms

So, you are not blessed with lithe limbs... all is not lost! Go for a sleeve just below the elbow – this usually covers the offending areas and leaves the most slender part of your arm on show.

Don't go for shiny fabrics – instead opt for matt, textured or lacy fabrics that do not reflect the light. A little shoulder padding can help to define a rounded or bulky shoulder but is best in a jacket or bolero rather than a dress (**21**).

Soft, fluted sleeves in drapey and floaty fabrics will detract from heavy arms and draw attention lower down the arm, perfect for showing off a really gorgeous bracelet and manicured nails (**22**).

Never wear puffed or capped sleeves – they will cut across your arms at the fullest part. And don't wear skinny straps – they will only draw attention to the fullness of your arms.

Problem skin and tattoos

A tattoo is one of the biggest statements of personal style, but you may not want it to be on show when you walk down the aisle. If you have a prominent tattoo you'd like to conceal, then how about wearing a lightweight cover-up in chiffon or tulle with a strategically placed lace motif or cluster of beading? It could provide the perfect disguise and add pretty details across shoulders or around arms.

The same idea applies if you are looking to disguise problem skin or even suntan marks. Go for a translucent, soft cover-up that subtly covers the bits you don't want showing – lace, chiffon, georgette and embroidered tulles are all good choices for this. Then really highlight your favourite areas, have a French polish and wear sparkly jewellery. Choose a dress style that really makes the most of your assets and no one will notice the bits you want to hide.

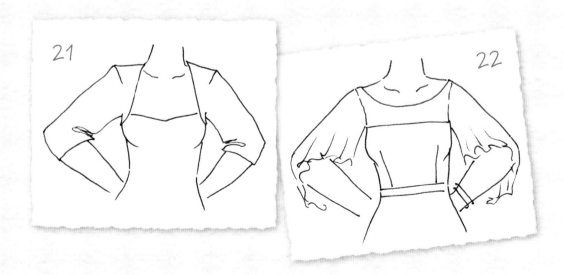

Good Foundations

Choosing the right underwear can go a long way to creating the ideal silhouette. A well-fitting bra and smoothing knickers will give you confidence and improve your posture. Go shopping for your undergarments before starting to construct or even measure up for your dress.

Let's talk bras...

A bra should fit quite tightly around the rib cage so that the fastening strap stays parallel to the ground and is not pulled upwards into an arch once the shoulder straps are on, but should not be so tight you can't breathe. The underwiring should literally cup right around the outline of the breast from under the armpit to between the breasts and should fit smoothly against the body. The cup should be filled but not so as to squeeze you out over the top (thus creating the double-boob effect). Get fitted properly – don't just go for what feels comfy; ask a professional.

A note on knickers

Let's be practical, ladies. A frilly bit of nonsense may be perfect for the wedding night but could create lumps and bumps beneath your beautifully fitted dress. Go for smooth-line knickers during the day and slip into something smaller in the evening.

If you opt for support knickers, bear in mind that if you are wearing a boned bodice it may not be possible to pull big knickers (or tights for that matter) up far enough to keep them smooth beneath your bodice. This needn't be a problem; just look out for holding-in knickers (and tights) that have a cutout crotch to allow you to go to the toilet.

Hosiery

Know your hosiery options and buy spares! Stockings are held up by hooks that hang down from a suspender belt that must be put on before knickers (you only make that mistake once, believe me). If you've never worn a belt, be sure to give it a trial run first, particularly if you are wearing clingy fabric over your thighs – the clips may show through, revealing unsightly bumps.

Hold-ups, secured with silicone or rubber grips, can provide a smoother solution and are usually more stretchy than stockings. However, they often only come in one size and the grips can aggravate sensitive skin.

Useful Tip

For many, the garter is an essential part of bridal attire. Traditionally worn around the thigh to stop stockings sliding down, many brides use this as their 'something blue'. Be sure it doesn't cause an unsightly bump in your fabric.

Sketching a Design

Before striding ahead and cutting into fabrics, it is worth sketching your dress to make sure it is a balanced, cohesive design that takes into account not only your body shape but also how you're going to move around as well as the environment in which you'll be seen.

Consider your venue

Is it grand or humble? Are you to be wed in the evening or at midday? Are there rules about what you can wear? If you are marrying in church they may insist you have your shoulders covered.

Take in all the angles

For most of the ceremony your guests will be seeing you from the back – make sure you've thought about this when designing your dress. Do you want to make a dramatic entrance and rustle all the way up the aisle in crisp layers of pristine silk? Or would you rather glide silently, swan-like, around your reception?

How will you dance in the evening? If you are having a long train, consider whether you'd like to wear your skirts hitched up into a bustle at the back or wear them looped up and tied elegantly to your wrist.

Sketch it out

Even if you are no good at drawing, just roughly sketch the silhouette of your design and play with the proportions between bodice, skirt, decoration and exposed skin. It is just as important to consider what's on show as well as what covers the rest. You could enlarge the model from page 41 on a photocopier and use her as a template.

Be creative

Gather inspirations all around you – anything from films, books, pictures in a magazine, even a piece of broken jewellery – all can evoke a feel.

The beauty of creating your own dress is that the little details – pearl buttons versus fabric-covered, for example, can be decided as you go along, but the overall style needs to be decided so as to avoid expensive mistakes with the wrong choice of fabric or hours wasted making embellishments that won't even be seen.

Choosing Fabric

This is a very personal decision and I recommend not overcrowding the process with too many people. You'll probably know the moment you see it what fabric you like, whether it be shiny or matt, floppy or crisp, plush or sheer. Here are the ones I use most.

Duchesse satin

A crisp fabric with a smooth, shiny surface on one side and a duller reverse. It has a crisp yet pliable texture that lends itself very well to full-skirted designs, especially those with soft pleats, folds and hitching. Duchesse satin is available in silk (shown below right), polyester and mixed fibres. Polyester has the benefit of being relatively crease-resistant and also much cheaper than silk. Silk, far more pricey, has a lustre second to none but be prepared for its softly crumpled surface texture – it also has a tendency to roll up at the edges once cut, so if you have your heart set on this fabric, look out for a non-roll variety that will be easier to work with.

Useful Tip

If you are buying a long length of fabric, ask the shop to put it back onto a roll for you – it will be easier to lay out when you come to cut out your dress and should eliminate the possibility of ugly creases.

ONLINE OR IN PERSON?

I cannot stress enough the importance of seeing, feeling and handling the fabrics for your bridal gown. If you visit fabric shops, the sales assistants can give you a much more personalized service, advising on the right fabric for your body shape, dress design and budget.
Use their expertise and experience, but don't be coerced into anything – always choose a fabric you love. If your idea of shopping is your laptop and a glass of wine, then you really must do your research, and, to avoid disappointment, be certain to only use reputable companies that will post you a sample. If you can't have a sample, check the returns policy before ordering.

LACE

Lace is a delicately woven, openwork fabric that is readily available in cotton, viscose, nylon, polyester and metallic fibres. It varies in price more than any other fabric and so really must be seen 'in the piece' before you buy. Lace can be much narrower than many fabrics, which adds to its expense – if your heart is set on a lace dress, but your budget won't stretch, consider using it to highlight areas of your design rather than all over, as featured in 'Florence', page 126.

Here are a few types of lace:

- Chantilly lace is a lightweight, delicate fabric, usually with a small design (**9**).
- Guipure lace is a dense, heavy lace with a glossy surface due to the long, silky fibres that adorn its surface.
- Broderie anglaise is not strictly lace but a lightweight fabric (such as cotton), with patterns cut out in a series of holes, the edges of which are finished with a satin stitch.
- All-over lace has an 'all-over' design, usually with a scalloped edge running down both sides of the fabric – this can be carefully trimmed and used to add decoration to the hem of a garment (see page 59).
- Corded lace is an all-over lace that has been embroidered with a fine cord highlighting the motifs (**10**).

Taffeta

This is a crisp, evenly woven fabric with a smooth surface texture and, regardless of fibre (usually silk or polyester), it has a subtle lustre (**1**). The plain weave of this fabric lends itself to 'shot' colours, which also brings out the soft crumpled appearance of this regal fabric. Due to its sculptural qualities, taffeta is wonderful for full-skirted designs, or details such as ruffles and bows, as it holds a shape. (Lady Diana Spencer wore silk taffeta when she wed Prince Charles in 1981.)

Chiffon and georgette

These soft, fine translucent fabrics are available in both synthetic and natural fibres. The heavier the fabric the more floppy it will be, rather than floaty. Georgette (**3**) is typically heavier than chiffon (**2**), with the fibres more tightly twisted in the weaving process making it springier and more crêpey that chiffon. Both fabrics require delicate handling and a huge amount of patience; not to sound discouraging, but it is best avoided by beginners. If you take the plunge then allow plenty of time – everything about working with chiffon and georgette takes longer.

TAFFETA: **1**
CHIFFON: **2**
GEORGETTE: **3**
DUPION SILK: **4**
SATIN-BACKED CRÊPE: **5**
SILK CHARMEUSE: **6**
HEAVY CRÊPE DE MAROCCAIN: **7**
ORGANZA: **8**
CHANTILLY LACE: **9**
CORDED LACE: **10**

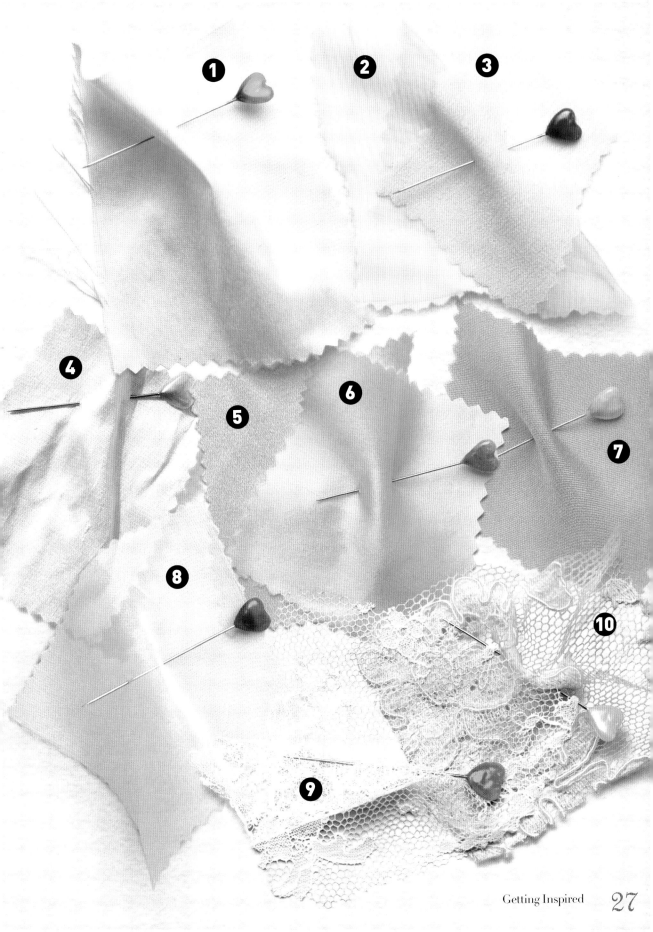

Dupion silk

Possibly available in more shades than any other fabric, dupion silk (**4**) is versatile and relatively inexpensive making it an extremely popular choice. It has a crisp texture with a soft sheen and slubby weave that adds interesting irregularities to the fabric. Many dupions come as a 'shot' fabric, where the fibres going across the weave are a different colour to those going up and down, giving a two-tone colour effect that becomes more extreme the more contrasting the two colours are.

Crêpe

This weave is available in a myriad of fibre choices: silk, wool, polyester, viscose and any variety of mixed fibres. Its distinctive quality, regardless of fibre content, is a matt, slightly crinkly surface texture and a floppy cloth with a good drape. For bridal wear, the most likely choice is a smoother silk or polyester crêpe such as crêpe de maroccain or crêpe de chine.

Crêpe de chine is a finely woven, very drapey fabric, perfect for slinky dresses and linings. Heavy crêpe de maroccain (**7**, page 27) is of a similar weave to crêpe de chine, only has a much denser texture and heavier flop (as shown in Pippa Middleton's dress at the Royal Wedding of the Duke and Duchess of Cambridge). Wool crêpe is also a beautiful fabric but more likely to be seen on the mother of the bride as a suit or a shift dress rather than as a bridal gown. Polyester or viscose crêpes, the budget alternatives to silk, have similar draping qualities but don't quite have the lustre of silk.

Satin-backed crêpe and charmeuse

These satins have all the draping qualities of the crêpes mentioned before but with the surface on one side being very smooth and glossy. They are hugely popular in bridal and evening gowns for their lustrous shine and wide range of colours. As ever, silk has the most luxurious qualities of all the satins available. It holds an intensity of colour not achievable in synthetic fibres and a drape far superior to its poorer relatives (**5** and **6**, page 27). There are some very good-quality polyester satins available on the market but be sure to shop around to get the best quality you can afford.

Organza

A stiff, crisp, sheer fabric with a fine and even but open gauzy weave, as with the dupion these are often 'shot', giving the two-tone effect. Its translucent nature means it is often used for sleeves, collars, ruffles and as an over layer on skirts. Organza has a relatively matt surface, although some of the synthetic versions are a bit shinier, with a 'crystal' effect – this can be pretty for flower girls and bridesmaids but use carefully as it can often look a bit 'fancy dress'.

Its crisp texture made it very popular in the 1950s for full-skirted designs and it is beautiful when layered with other fabrics of the same or contrasting colour. Fabulous effects can be created by using many layers of organza in different colours, perhaps graduating from light to dark through many layers of a full skirt (**8**, page 27).

INTERLINING, INTERFACING AND TOILE FABRICS

With none of the glamour of silks and satins, these essential fabrics often go overlooked, as by their very nature they are invisible in the finished garment. But ignore them at your peril – interfacings, interlinings and a toile (pronounced 'twaarl') are all part of a beautiful, fitted dress.

■ Interlining

This is a layer of fabric that lies sandwiched between the outer and lining fabric and is usually stitched directly to the individual pieces of either the lining or the outer fabric (this is called mounting). From then on the mounted fabrics are treated as one layer. In this book we use interlining to add a little stability to bodices but you may also choose to interline your entire dress.

Any fabric that is sandwiched between outer fabric and lining can be called an interlining or underlining, and it comes in all weights and thicknesses to serve many different purposes, so don't expect shops to have a specific section. Just be clear about what you wish to achieve and ask for a suitable material for the task in hand.

■ Interfacing

This is a woven or mesh fabric, often with an adhesive iron-on surface on one side. It helps to stabilize the texture of a fabric, strengthening it, making it slightly stiffer and preventing treated areas of a garment from stretching.

Available in fusible and sew-in, and in a huge range of weights and thicknesses, it is essential to choose the correct interfacing for your fabric. For most projects, a soft 'hand' or 'handle', light- to medium-weight, fusible interfacing does the job and can always be layered up to increase stiffness and stability. Apply interfacing to the wrong side of your fabric – 'sew in' should be tacked to the piece of fabric within the seam allowance (as you would when 'mounting' fabrics), and 'fusible' should be applied with a steam iron, set to the temperature suitable for your fabric.

Interfacing is generally only available in white and charcoal, so don't worry that you can't find a colour to match your dress fabric. When you choose your fabrics, ask the sales assistant for their advice on the correct interfacing.

■ Toile fabrics

When making your toile – the mock-up of your wedding gown and in particular the bodice – it is best to use a cheaper fabric that you can work easily with to adjust and fit to your shape. In this book, we use calico (also known as muslin or quilter's cotton), a 100% cotton fabric with a plain weave and very little natural stretch. It is a good idea to have a supply of this fabric at all times, for making mock-ups and practising tricky techniques. For more on making your toile, see page 44.

Antiquing Fabric

Materials with a high natural fibre content, such as cotton, linen and silk, can be successfully dyed to look vintage – here, I have used tea for the lace bolero on page 156, but coffee is just as effective, producing a more yellow tone.

1

2

1 Make sure the vessel you use is plenty big enough for the entire piece of fabric or garment to be submerged and stirred. Using approximately two regular tea bags per two pints (litre) of water, make a brew using boiling water – leave for a few minutes and then remove the tea bags to avoid patchiness in the mixture, and stirring to evenly distribute the colour. Allow to cool, then add your fabric or garment.

2 Remove the lace and rinse thoroughly with cold water. Dry a section to test the colour and repeat until you achieve the colour you desire. Once dry, iron your fabric from the back, using a pressing cloth, to avoid making the fabric surface shiny.

Useful Tip

The colour you will achieve depends on the colour of the existing garment, the length of time it is in the brew and the fibre content. With the viscose/cotton lace I have used, I left the material (which was white) in the mixture for five minutes before it reached the ideal colour.

Embellishments & Jewellery

You may wish to create a sleek, simple and no-frills gown, but adding a little embellishment or jewellery is a wonderful opportunity to make your dress totally unique and stamp your personal style on an outfit.

Flowers

Purchased or handmade fabric flowers can add a romantic, whimsical feel. They work best when placed asymmetrically and used in clusters or when nestled amongst folds or hitches in the fabric (see page 76 for how to make a fabric corsage or rosebud).

Lace

Lace motifs can be purchased as ready-to-apply bridal decorations, complete with beading and sequins, but it can be even more special to create your own by carefully cutting motifs from an all-over lace fabric (see page 27). Shapes can then be overlapped and decorated with beads, sequins and crystals to make a design that is individual to you.

Beads, pearls, sequins and crystals

These can all add glamour and radiance to a dress. Consider what time of day you are to be wed and what effect the lighting may have on the sparkle. At a candlelit wedding you can go to town with the glitz, but for a midday beach wedding, all-over sparkle could look tacky, and you don't want to blind the guests!

Useful Tip

If you are set on wearing Grandma's pearls with your wedding dress, it is worth taking this into consideration when planning any embellishments. A bodice encrusted with crystals may overpower a delicate string of pearls, making them appear discoloured or insignificant. However, a simpler design, perhaps one incorporating pearl details, would enhance them.

Jewellery

Think about the jewellery you may want to wear. Perhaps you have a gift from your fiancé that you couldn't be wed without, or your 'something old' is a family heirloom. With bridal jewellery, less is usually more, but this doesn't mean boring; you can still wear chandelier earrings, just perhaps not with the matching necklace, rings, cuff and nose stud.

Getting Started

'My designs are known for their beautiful ornamentation, details, fabrics, and embroideries – which are never more important than on a wedding dress.'

OSCAR DE LA RENTA, FASHION DESIGNER

Equipment & Materials

Clear yourself a peaceful, clean space to work, lock out unwanted helpers (especially those with muddy paws), and have all your tools and equipment to hand so you don't have to stop and hunt about. We're ready to get started!

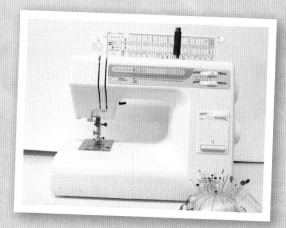

Sewing machine

There are bargains to be had on the Internet, but be very careful – don't buy a machine with a service guarantee if you then have to pay a fortune in shipping to get it back for repairs and servicing.

Your sewing machine

You will need a basic sturdy sewing machine that has a straight stitch and a zigzag stitch – anything else is a bonus but not needed to produce the dress or follow the instructions in this book. There are many machines on the market that offer a vast array of embroidery stitches and computerized sequences but – unless you are doing decorative fancy stitching on craft projects – the novelty will quickly wear off and you'll only use the basic stitches.

If you are about to purchase a machine then I'd recommend going to a local supplier who can offer servicing and repairs. You should then be able to test drive the machine and get a feel for it.

Dress stand

A dress stand needn't be expensive, although – as with most things – you get what you pay for. If you can, choose a solid stand, or dummy, as the adjustable dummies can be a bit flimsy. With a solid stand, be sure to choose one that is no bigger than you are, and which has a fabric covering to allow you to pin directly onto it. Both types of stands can be padded out to represent your shape. I often use a bra with padding to get a more realistic bust; layers of quilter's wadding layered up can also be useful to get curves in the right places!

Dress stand

OVERLOCKER OR SERGER

By no means essential and, if you are just starting out, don't get one until you are totally at ease with a sewing machine, as overlockers are notoriously tricky to get threaded and tensioned correctly. If you have been dressmaking for some time however, get one – it will change your life! Overlockers are primarily used for neatening seam allowances, hemming and in the construction of stretch garments. They can also be used to attach elastic and stretch trimmings.

Iron and ironing board with heat-reflective cover

Choose a good-quality steam iron and then only use filtered or special de-ionized iron water. You don't want scale deposits discharging all over your beautiful dress. You will also need a pressing cloth (a clean, white cotton handkerchief does the job) and pressing aid for getting into the curves. If you have a tailor's ham or a sleeve board these will also be very handy. If not, you could make a pressing aid by tightly stuffing a clean, white cotton sock with toy stuffing and then stitch up the open end. This can then be used to get into the sleeves and curved seams when pressing those tricky shapes.

Shears, snips and paper scissors

Buy the best pair of scissors you can afford, and then keep them under lock and key. Fabric shears should never be used for cutting paper, hair or anything other than fabric. You will also need a separate pair of snips for cutting threads and scissors for cutting paper (these needn't be fancy).

Good-quality pins

You may think pins are pins, but when working with bridal fabrics it is important to get pins that are very fine and sharp. Imagine the heartbreak of a blunt old pin snagging your wedding dress! Plain-headed pins are perfect for satins, chiffons and other fine, smooth fabrics but you may also like to have glass-headed pins for lace and netting, as they are easier to see and handle in these textured materials.

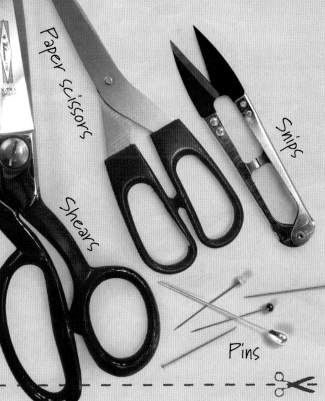

Paper scissors

Shears

Snips

Pins

Thread

For hand finishing, cotton or even silk threads are softer and silkier than polyester and tend to blend more invisibly into a finished garment (this is why they are so popular for quilting and crafting).

Haberdashery

Often overlooked as secondary to your bridal gown's outer fabric, haberdashery items (or notions) can be the underpinnings of any well-made dress. If chosen wisely, they can elevate a garment to a whole new level.

Collecting haberdashery can also be such a pleasure – as well as buying the essential items for your current project, look out for interesting and unusual items such as embellished zips or embroidered ribbons. Visit haberdashers and flea markets alike, looking for any unusual and eye-catching finds – who knows what gems may be hiding in all those little drawers and tins.

Zips

In addition to regular 'dress', zips are available in 'open ended' and 'invisible' and come with metal or plastic teeth. In this book we will be using invisible zips, which are always plastic. If purchasing a zip for your dress, make sure to get the best colour match to your fabric, and always buy a zip at least as long as the opening it is to be sewn into. Long zips can be easily shortened. See page 74 for how to insert an invisible zip.

Thread

Your thread colour and garment must match. To be certain of this, you must, in daylight, unwind a few inches of thread and lay it across your fabric's surface for proper scrutiny before purchasing anything. A good-quality polyester 'sew-all' thread is suitable for most sewing – it is very strong but also has a small amount of stretch, which means it will flex with the body.

For your overlocker, choose large, colour-matched rolls of a less-expensive polyester thread, as you will use miles of the stuff! Check that the texture is smooth and matt, not too shiny and not hairy, as this could snag and break.

For satin-stitched hems (see page 61), I tend to use viscose machine embroidery thread for a more decorative finish. It is readily available and has a lovely, glossy appearance. It snags more easily than regular threads, so I tend to use it only on the first looper of my overlocker so that it shows on the outside of a finished garment.

Tapes and ribbons

Shoulder and bust pads

This is for those who may be looking to boost their assets! Typically made from soft, breathable foam or wadding and available in all sorts of sizes, these pads are available from any good sewing shops and tend to only come in black or white. They should be invisible in a finished garment; however, if you get a colour shadow showing through, use a piece of your own fabric to cover the pad before sewing it in.

Tapes and ribbons

Having a collection of even short lengths of tape and ribbon can be handy. They can be used to stabilize seams (especially shoulder seams), bind hems (as with bias binding, see page 54), or can be used practically to hang a garment from the inside seams rather than from its delicate straps.

Buttons

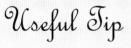

Useful Tip

Before throwing worn-out clothes away, give them the quick once over and remove any useful buttons, braid or shoulder pads. Just add them to your collection – you never know when they could come in handy.

Buttons

Ooh, where to start... I love buttons! Buttons needn't just be a method of fastening your clothes – they can add a decorative focal point to your dress and, if you love hunting in charity shops, you may find some beauties. The dresses in this book use fabric-covered buttons, which add a sophisticated and professional finish to handcrafted garments. See page 70 for how to attach different types of buttons.

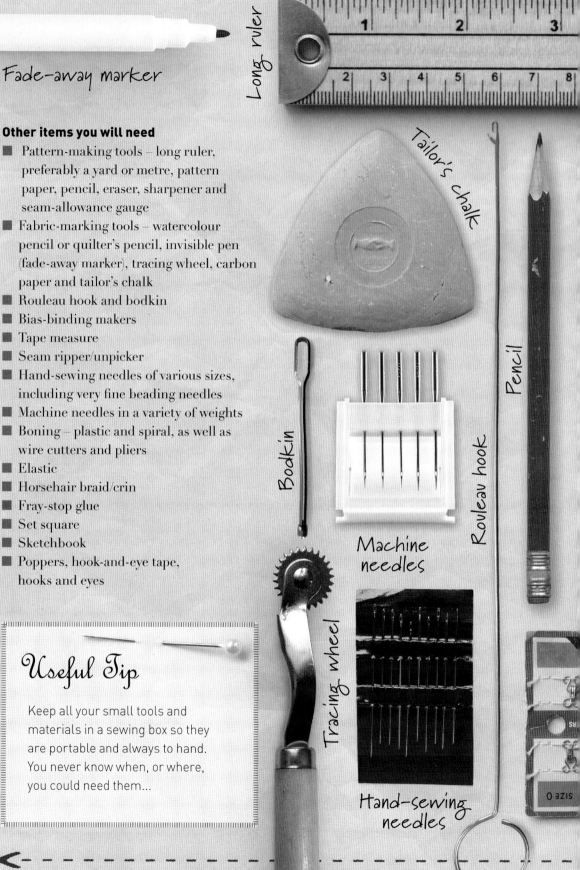

Fade-away marker

Long ruler

Tailor's chalk

Pencil

Bodkin

Machine needles

Rouleau hook

Tracing wheel

Hand-sewing needles

Other items you will need

- Pattern-making tools – long ruler, preferably a yard or metre, pattern paper, pencil, eraser, sharpener and seam-allowance gauge
- Fabric-marking tools – watercolour pencil or quilter's pencil, invisible pen (fade-away marker), tracing wheel, carbon paper and tailor's chalk
- Rouleau hook and bodkin
- Bias-binding makers
- Tape measure
- Seam ripper/unpicker
- Hand-sewing needles of various sizes, including very fine beading needles
- Machine needles in a variety of weights
- Boning – plastic and spiral, as well as wire cutters and pliers
- Elastic
- Horsehair braid/crin
- Fray-stop glue
- Set square
- Sketchbook
- Poppers, hook-and-eye tape, hooks and eyes

Useful Tip

Keep all your small tools and materials in a sewing box so they are portable and always to hand. You never know when, or where, you could need them...

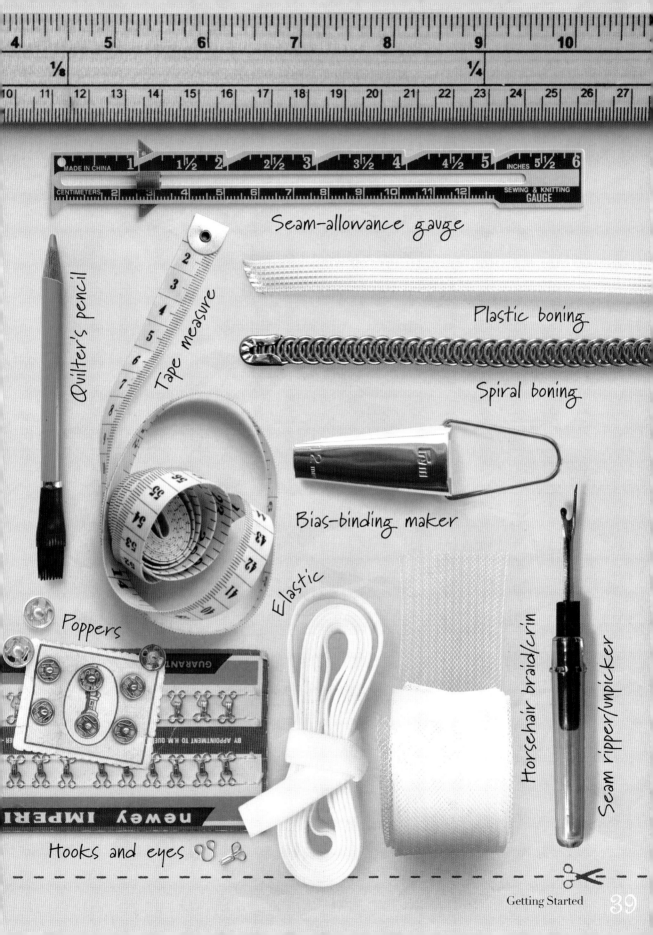

Seam-allowance gauge

Plastic boning

Spiral boning

Quilter's pencil

Tape measure

Bias-binding maker

Poppers

Elastic

Horsehair braid/crin

Seam ripper/unpicker

Hooks and eyes

Getting Measured Up

Few things could be more important when it comes to making your own dress than having a beautifully fitted garment with a gorgeous silhouette. And for this, you need accurate measurements and good underwear.

Before heading to the section on making your chosen dress, you must ensure you get the best possible fit on your special day – this means measuring yourself, adjusting the pattern pieces found at the back of the book and making a bodice toile to be extra certain of your fit before you begin to draw up the pattern particular to your dress.

If you are considering wearing a padded bra, support knickers or even a corset, be sure to wear them whilst measuring yourself – after all, they are there to adjust your natural shape and could have a big effect.

Taking measurements
On the right are the basic measurements you will need for the bodice patterns at the back of the book and to draw your own patterns for your chosen skirt.

Useful Tip

If in doubt about where to measure your waistline, do the 'I'm a little teapot' motions – when you bend to the side, your waist is the bit that creases!

- **Bust (B)** All the way around your body at the fullest part of your bust, level with your nipples.
- **Under Bust (UB)** Directly beneath your bust, around your rib cage.
- **Waist (W)** Most people naturally take their waist measurement a little too low. Your natural waist is above your tummy button between the bottom of your rib cage and the top of your hip bone.
- **Upper Hips (UH)** Around your hip bones.
- **Lower Hips (LH)** Around the fullest part of your bottom.
- **Nape to Waist (NW)** From the knobbly bone at the base of your neck to your waistline, straight down your back.
- **Waist to Upper Hip (WUH)** From your waistline to your upper hip bone, down your side.
- **Waist to Lower Hip (WLH)** From your waistline to your lower hip line, down your side.
- **Waist to Hem (W/HEM)** Allow for high heels if wearing a dress to the ground.
- **Across Front (AF)** Across the chest between the natural creases of the body to armpit.
- **Across Back (AB)** Across shoulder blades between the natural line crease of body to armpit.

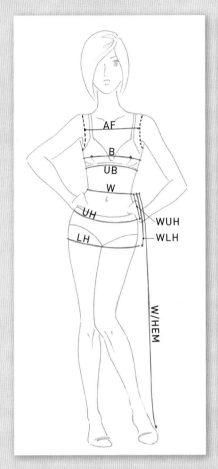

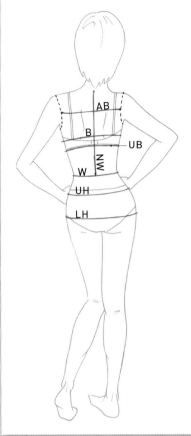

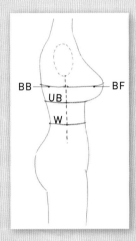

Detailed bust measurement

To make the most of the patterns in this book, we need to take a more detailed bust measurement. This will be especially relevant to you if you are small framed but busty, as you will be proportionately bigger across the front than you are across the back.

First, tie a ribbon or piece of elastic around your bust at the fullest part, making sure that the ribbon stays parallel to the floor all the way around the body. It should be not too loose or it will drop.

Mark the ribbon or elastic directly beneath the centre of your armpit on each side then measure your bust again from side to side across the front and across the back between the markings. Make a note of these two new measurements. We'll call these **Bust Front (BF)** and **Bust Back (BB)**.

If you are fortunate enough to have use of a dress stand, now is the time to adjust it to equal your measurements. To pad the bust, use an old bra and pad it up to equal your bust size and shape.

Wrap layers of wadding around the waist and hips until the measurements tally with your own. Put a snug fitting T-shirt or vest over the wadding to hold it all in place, check measurements again and adjust if necessary.

How to Use the Patterns

The patterns in this book do not represent any specific dress size you may find in the shops – they merely map your basic measurements and so can be used to draw up your own personal pattern, rather than pigeonholing you into a commercial 'size'.

Sketching it out

Rather than drawing directly onto the patterns provided at the back of the book, I suggest placing tracing paper over the top and working onto it so that any errors are easier to amend. Stick both layers of paper down at the corners so they don't slip about.

To draft a basic bodice pattern you will need the measurements taken for your Bust (B), including Bust Front (BF) and Back Bust (BB), Underbust (UB), Waist (W) and Upper Hips (UH) (see page 40). The bodice is made up of four panels: front, side front, back and side back. These four panels will represent half of your body (they will later be cut from folded fabric to achieve an entire bodice).

1 Working your way down the four bodice pieces on the pattern sheets, choose the appropriate line for each of your measurements and mark these points as dots.

2 Now sketch a line that joins all the dots. A flexible curve may be useful if you are not confident sketching freehand. Your line may cross over several of the original lines on the provided patterns. Don't worry, we are all different. Some of you may cross over lots of lines, others may cross none.

3 Draw in the upper and lower edges that correspond with the B and UH lines you have drawn.

NOTES ON THE PATTERN SHEETS

■ There are no pattern pieces provided for skirts, but detailed instructions on how to draw your own are included in the instructions for each dress. This way you have control over the length and fullness of your skirts, and they can be tailored to suit your fabric, style and body shape.

■ The upper bodice pattern is specific to Amélie, and instructions for its use are included on page 92.

■ The bolero jacket pattern is an additional garment and instructions on how to make it are found on page 156.

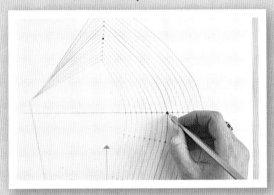

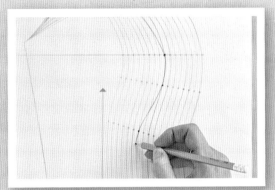

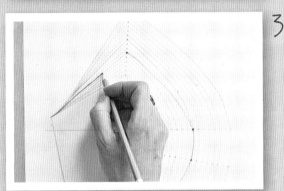

4 At this point, you may need to lengthen or shorten your bodice pattern. Use your Nape to Waist (NW) measurement and Waist to Upper Hip (WUH) measurement to determine whether this is necessary. As a guide, half of your NW measurement will be approximately equal to the distance between the Bust (B) line and Waist (W) line on the pattern. To shorten, slice the pattern along the double lines and overlap the two pieces as necessary. To lengthen, slice the pattern and add a piece of paper behind, extending the pattern lines as necessary.

Preparing the pattern pieces

5 Once you have drawn your bodice pieces, you need to make them fit for use as patterns. Transfer all the grain and number markings from the provided pattern sheets, marking the B, UB and W lines as a notch at the point where they meet the outer edge on your pattern piece.

Add ⅝in (1.5cm) seam allowance to all sides of each pattern piece (except the centre-front edge of the centre-front panel), using a seam allowance gauge. The original lines are the intended stitching lines.

Now that you have created your own bodice pattern, your next step is to make a toile.

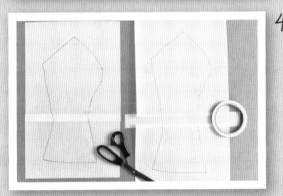

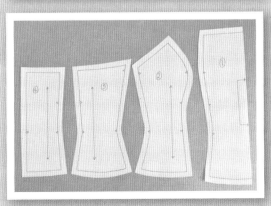

Making a Toile

A toile is a mock-up garment, most often in calico, that you can fit and alter before committing to the final fabric. This will give you a perfectly fitting bodice to use as the template for your chosen dress. Any alterations you make can then be used to adjust your basic bodice pattern, so you can be confident that your wedding dress will fit perfectly.

1

2

3

Basic bodice toile

1 Fold your toile fabric (I suggest a medium-weight calico) in half, selvedge to selvedge, as shown. Lay out your personalized pattern pieces (see page 42), ensuring that the grainlines on the pattern run exactly parallel to the selvedge and fold edges.

2 The centre-front panel should be laid directly on the fold so, once cut, it opens out like a butterfly. Pin and cut out the fabric.

3 Mark the seam lines by tracing around the stitch line onto the wrong side of the fabric (see page 43 for guidance on adding

seam allowances). Mark all the notches you drew earlier on your personalized pattern, as they will help when you are constructing the garment.

4 Using plastic boning (see page 67 for more on this), zigzag stitch bones down the centre of each panel, following the grain of the fabric. Matching stitching lines and notches, pin and stitch the side front, side and side-back seams. Use a long stitch so that seams can be unpicked quickly. Leave the centre back open.

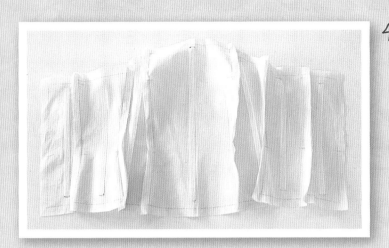

4

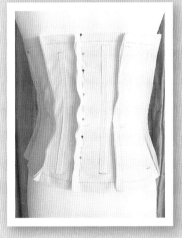

5

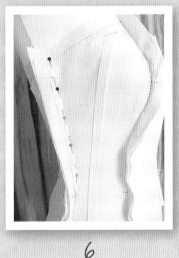

6

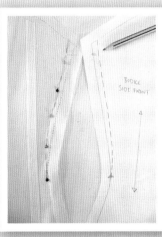

7

5 Try on your bodice inside out, getting your sewing buddy to pin down the centre-back stitching line.

6 Now it's time to make any adjustments to the fit. First, pinch any excess fabric into the seams and pin, as shown. If any areas feel too tight or the seam looks to be straining, use an unpicker to open the seam and pin a new line for a better fit.

Refer also to 'Notes on Fitting' on page 46 for more information on adjusting your toile.

7 If you have made alterations to your toile, draw on your toile bodice, along the new lines, with pen or pencil and then unpick the seams. Transfer any new lines onto the corresponding bodice pattern pieces as shown, then trim or add to the seam allowances as necessary.

If you make drastic changes to the original pattern, you may wish to make another toile to check the fit. Repeat as necessary. Once you have a perfectly fitting bodice, mark each pattern piece so as not to get muddled with previous drafts.

NOTES ON FITTING

■ When making alterations to any garment, work from the shoulders down (there is no point in getting a perfect hem only to lift the entire dress from the shoulders).

■ Be sure to wear the same undies and height of shoes as you will wear with your finished dress.

■ Check armholes or underarm bodice edges for a smooth and comfortable fit – too tight and there will be unsightly bulges, too loose and you'll feel very exposed.

■ Check the bust – make sure you are happy with the shape of curved seams and with the overall silhouette.

■ Check that the waist is a flattering fit and that the seams want to flow smoothly. This is where any unwanted length in the bodice will become apparent – pin away any excess length until you achieve a neat-looking waistline.

■ Check the fit over hips and bottom – make sure it is comfortable to sit and stand, remembering you may be getting in and out of a low car seat.

■ Try to make any adjustments to your toile symmetrical, but if you know that you have a lopsided figure just ensure that, when making adjustments to your pattern, you draw a pattern piece to represent each part of the bodice. This means that each piece will be cut singly and not on folded fabric – and ensure that each piece is clearly marked for the left and right-hand sides of your body.

■ Give the toile a test drive – wave your arms around, practise a hug, sit, crouch, bend over, wiggle your hips – do anything you might do on the dancefloor! This dress has to see you through the most important day of your life – you don't want any wardrobe malfunctions.

■ You can make a toile of your entire dress, including the long skirt, if you want. After drawing and cutting patterns for your dress design as indicated for each of the dresses in the book, make a single layer mock-up of all the main components of the dress, sewing together all the main seams, but leave out any unnecessary details such as seam finishes, plackets, and fastenings.

■ If you have previous experience of dressmaking and feel confident in your pattern drawing skills, then perhaps make up the skirt toile in your lining fabric to reduce wastage.

■ Check skirts for fullness and length – chop off any excessive length, leaving just a couple of inches (5cm) longer than you'd like the finished skirt to be.

Preparing your Dress Fabric

Fabrics are treated when manufactured to keep them looking great in the shops; many will soften or shrink when washed or steamed with an iron. They also tend to distort when put on the roll for sale. Here we address how to prepare your fabric for cutting.

How much fabric?

Once you have a perfectly fitting toile, and any alterations have been transferred to your patterns, unpick the toile's seams and use the pieces as a guide to help you work out how much fabric to purchase for your dress. You will need to know the widths of the fabrics you want to use in order to calculate how many yards (or metres) to buy.

Cutting your dress fabric

Before laying your pattern, you must straighten the ends of the fabric and then check the alignment of the grain. Woven fabrics consist of two sets of threads that run at right angles to each other. The long threads that run up and down are called the warp and the shorter threads that run from side to side are the weft.

1 If your fabric is of an evenly and tightly woven texture it should be possible to tear it. Make a snip through the selvedge with scissors and then, holding either side of the snip, rip across towards the opposite selvedge. If the strip of fabric tears off before reaching the other side, make another snip and repeat as necessary.

2 If the idea of tearing your fabric scares the life out of you, or you have a loosely woven or decoratively woven fabric (such as jacquard or brocade), then we will draw a thread to get the straight grain. Snip the selvedge and grasp a single, crosswise thread and pull gently until the thread loosens or the fabric puckers. Push the puckered fabric across to the opposite selvedge, and cut along this line.

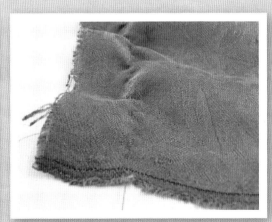

3

4

5

3 Lay your straightened fabric onto a square-cornered table or a cutting board, checking that the corners of the fabric are at a right angle.

4 If the corners of your fabric do not form right angles you will need to pull the fabric diagonally to correct the distortion. Grab hold of the edges diagonally and pull gently but firmly (possibly with the help of another person) until the crossing fibres are perpendicular.

5 If you pull your fabric diagonally (on the bias) you will notice it will stretch or give. We will use fabric cut on the bias to create rouleau (page 71), and bias binding (**5**) (see page 54). As it is cut diagonally, the fabric becomes flexible in all directions, allowing us to create a professional finish even around tricky curves. Once the grainlines are all straight, you are ready to lay the pattern pieces, pin them down and cut your fabric.

Useful Tips

If you are using chiffon or georgette, lay your pattern beneath the fabric and trace the outlines and markings onto the surface before cutting out.

Once cut, save all your scraps and practise each process until you are happy with your technique at each stage of construction. You may need to tweak the thread tensions, or adjust the feed dog on your sewing machine. Check your machine's instruction booklet for advice.

Seam Basics

Sewing the perfect seam is fundamental not only for constructing your wedding dress but for any dressmaking project. Be sure to do a test run on scraps of all your wedding dress fabrics, to check that thread tensions, machine needles and stitch lengths are all correct before working on your actual dress.

1

2a

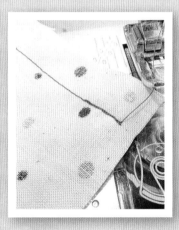

2b

Straight seams

1 Most sewing machines have markings on the plate to help you keep seam allowances accurate – keep the raw edges of the seam allowance level with the ⅝in (1.5cm) marking (this is the allowance used in most commercial patterns and is what we will be using in this book unless indicated otherwise). If your machine doesn't have this, then stick a strip of masking tape onto the plate, the edge being ⅝in (1.5cm) from the needle position.

2 Fabrics should be pinned right sides together (unless using a French seam, see page 55) and the cut edges should be flush to ensure an accurate seam allowance. Pins should be placed along the desired stitch line, pointing towards the sewing machine, giving you easy access to the pinheads so as to remove pins as you sew (**2a**). Seams should be backstitched at the beginning and end of each seam for reinforcement – ⅜in (1cm) should be sufficient (**2b**).

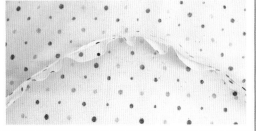

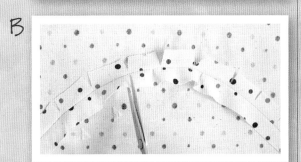

Curved seams

A curved seam joins two separate pieces of fabric that curve in a precise relationship to each other. Once sewn accurately they will lay smoothly over the contours of the body. Notches and markings on a pattern help you achieve this beautiful, 3D form. Take extra care to mark and match pieces accurately.

Curved seams can be confusing for new dressmakers, so practise on scraps. The outer edge of a curved seam will probably be longer than the actual stitch line of the seam, as when we add a seam allowance the outer curve will increase in length. When pinning and stitching a curved seam, do not be surprised if the seam allowances do not seem to match (**A**). As long as the line at which you will stitch is lying smoothly, all will be ok.

To press the seam allowances of a curved seam open, they must be snipped first. Cut little wedges of fabric from the inside of the curve to reduce bulk (**B**).

Understitching a seam

An understitch is a line of straight stitching that catches seam allowances down to the lining or facing of a garment. It gives a crisp edge to neckline and armhole openings and stops the lining or facing from peeking out along finished edges.

1 Prepare the seam by pressing allowances towards the lining or facing, clipping if necessary, then pinning from the right side of the fabric, through all layers of the seam allowance and lining or facings, except the outer layer. Stitch close to the seam line, on the facing or lining, through all layers of the seam allowance and inside fabric.

If the inner fabric is very fine, the stitching can be ⅛in (2–3mm); for heavy and thick fabrics, stitch further from the seam line, up to ¼in (5mm).

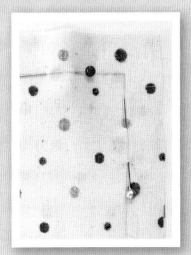
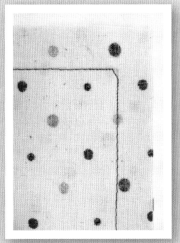
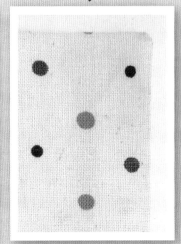

Sewing a perfect corner

1 To achieve a sharp point in a collar or sash, or anything that is to be turned inside out, you must stitch diagonally across the point. For this, pin your fabrics right sides facing, mark the exact shape you wish to achieve onto the wrong side of the fabric as accurately as possible (this is especially important if trying to achieve symmetry).

2 Stitch along your drawn line to ⅜in (1cm) short of the point, shorten the stitch length, then continue to ⅛in (2–3mm) short of the corner, pivot, then stitch diagonally across the corner with a few stitches (the thicker the fabric, the more stitches you will need), once back on the drawn line, pivot again and continue to stitch – after ⅜in (1cm), return stitch length back to normal.

3 Trim the excess fabric from the seam allowances, turn and press.

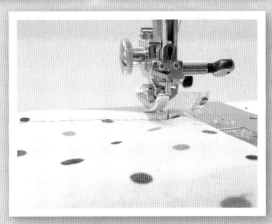

A

Topstitched corners

To get a perfect corner when topstitching, stitch right to the corner point, leave the needle down, pivot, then continue sewing in your new direction (**A**).

Seam Finishes

A perfect seam requires a perfect finish. Depending upon the fabric that you use and the location of the seam within the garment, there are a variety of ways that the raw edges can be treated.

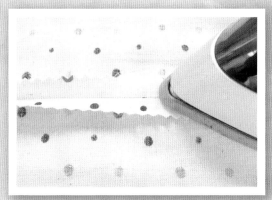

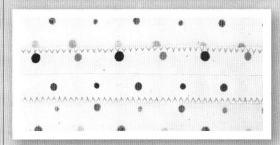

Pinked

This finish tapers the blunt cut edge of your fabric to reduce the bulk on a seam. Once you have stitched your seam, trim the edge of the seam allowance with pinking shears and press open (**A**).

Useful Tip

On heavier fabrics, it can be easier to finish the edge of pieces before constructing a seam – just make a note of how much fabric is trimmed, then adjust your stitching position to the reduced seam allowance.

Zigzagged

This finish will prevent fraying on internal seams and is especially useful on the seams where there may be friction. Stitch alongside each edge of the seam allowances using a medium-length and medium-width zigzag stitch (**B**). Press seam allowances open (**C**). This finish is only really used in the absence of an overlocker, or for an area too small to get into with an overlocker.

D

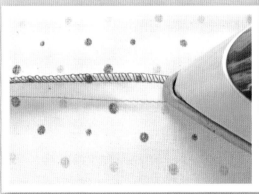

E

F

Overlocked

This finish is used to prevent fraying on internal seams, even on stretch fabrics. If you don't have an overlocker (serger), then look to see if your sewing machine has an 'overlock' stitch and follow the instructions for stitch length and width. Overlockers will cut and then overstitch a raw seam edge, so be extra careful when trimming already constructed seams, as unpicking overlocking is very time consuming – best to get it right the first time. For lightweight fabrics, you may want to overlock the seam allowances together (**D**) and then press to one side (**E**).

Seams on net

The edges on net will not fray or unravel, so they can be treated differently to other woven fabrics. This technique also reduces bulk in the seam. Lay one piece of net over the other so that they overlap an equal amount along the length of the seam. Stitch down the middle of this overlap, making a backstitch at each end – take extra care with net that the seam does not become stretched (**F**).

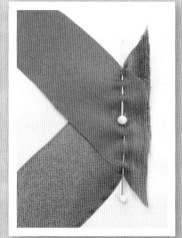

Bias bound

A beautiful finish on unlined garments, especially on those fabrics where the insides show, such as open-weave lace.

1 Cut equal width strips across the bias of your fabric (the width will depend on the size of your bias binding tool and could be anything between 1 and 2 inches (2.5–5cm).

2 Make a long continuous piece of binding by joining the strips together, right sides facing, and stitch diagonally on the straight grain.

3 Press seams open and trim off the excess (**3a**), then feed the bias strip into the binding maker, pressing the fabric as it emerges (**3b**).

4 Press the bias binding in half along its length, keeping folded edges flush. Slot the raw seam edge into the bias binding groove and fold the binding over it. Stitch close to the edge of the binding, catching both folded edges (**4a**). Seams can either be bound individually and pressed open or bound together and pressed to one side.

3b

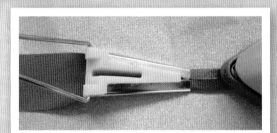

4a

Alternative method

For a finer, handfinished bound edge, first machine stitch the binding onto the edge, right side facing, along one of the grooves in the binding (closest to the raw edge). Then fold the binding round the raw edge of the fabric and slip stitch the folded edge neatly by hand on the inside (see page 62).

1a

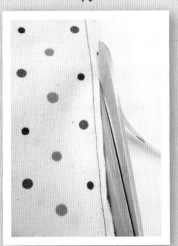
1b

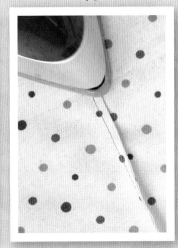
1c

French seams

Best used to finish sheer fabrics such as chiffon, georgette and organza. This is the only seam used in this book where the initial seam is stitched with the wrong sides facing.

1 Lay fabrics wrong side together and make a seam with the stitch line at ⅜in (1cm) seam allowance (**1a**), then trim allowance down to ⅛in (2–3mm) (**1b**) and press to one side (**1c**).

2

2 Press again, this time with right sides together, making sure that the stitching line is right on the edge of the fold.

3a

3 Stitch the seam again, this time at ¼in (5mm), enclosing the existing seam allowances (**3a**) then press the seam to one side (**3b**).

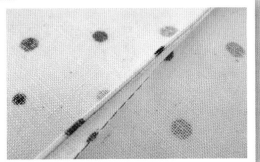
3b

Hems

A hem is usually the last job when finishing a garment. You can only achieve a perfect hem by trying your dress on and getting someone else to mark the desired hem length for you – this bit can't really be done alone.

With the wedding dress on, all the correct underwear and petticoats and your bridal shoes, it's time to try your dress for it's final fitting! Hitch the organza overlay up and out of the way in order to concentrate on the main skirt fabric and the dress hem. Pin the fabric at the point it hits the ground, all the way across the front panel of the skirt. If your dress has a train, start to angle the line of pins down as you travel across the side front panels so that the hem line flows into that glorious train. If you are not having a train, then simply continue to pin the skirt at ground level all the way round.

Once you have the floor level marked, you can decide how far above the ground you'd like the skirt to sit. I would recommend around ¾in (2cm) rather than having it actually touching the floor, but you must be prepared to walk more slowly and smoothly than you might normally. If you are wearing decorative shoes, 1½in (4cm) above the floor will show them off. Lay the dress on your working surface, and tack along the actual finished hemline.

The following hems may be used for the three dresses in this book.

Topstitch hem
This is probably the most durable of all hems (commonly seen on jeans), so it is perfect for linings. Trim the hem allowance to 1in (2.5cm) longer than finished length. Turn allowance twice, by ½in (12mm) each time, pin and press (**1**). Topstitch close to the folded edge with a straight stitch on the sewing machine (**2**).

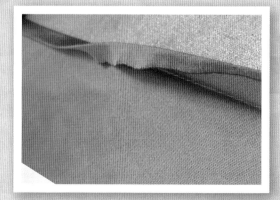

1

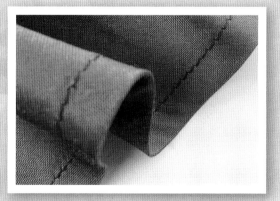

2

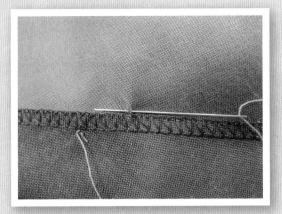

1

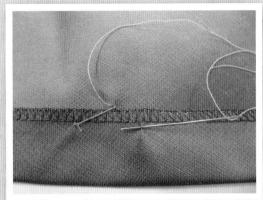

2a

Herringbone hem

This is a quick and relatively durable hand-sewn hem technique – it is great for sewing full hems but, as the stitches show on the inside, it can snag. It is best used where the hem will then be enclosed by the lining (using a slip stitch, for example – page 62).

1 Finish the raw edge with overlocking, pinking, zigzag stitch or binding. Press the hem allowance up, using a seam gauge to ensure the turning is even, then pin the turning into place.

Stitches flow from left to right, but the needle always points left (reverse this if you are left-handed). Secure your thread to the hem allowance, preferably starting at a seam, then take a tiny stitch in the garment, as shown, catching just a few fibres directly above the finished edge, then move across ⅜in (1cm) to the right.

2 Taking another tiny stitch, this time in the hem (**2a**), continue this process, alternating between hem and garment. Keep the stitches even in length (**2b**).

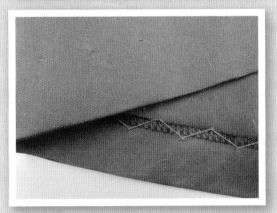

2b

Useful Tip

If you are wearing jewelled or beaded shoes, be careful to choose a finish where all the stitches are encased in the hem – diamanté and exposed stitches equal a snagged hem.

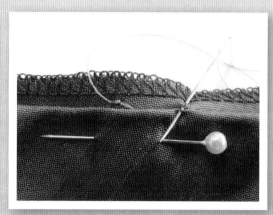

Lockstitch or hand blind hemming

This is a strong and virtually invisible hand-sewn hem, perfect where you want the added weight of a turned hem, without a row of stitches showing.

1 Finish the raw edge and press the hem allowance, as done for the herringbone hem. Stitches flow from left to right, with the edge of the hem allowance peeled back to reveal the wrong side of the fabric, then pinned back on itself.

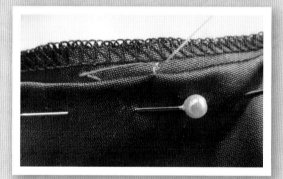

2 Fasten your thread on the hem allowance then, in one motion, take a tiny stitch, catching a few threads in the hem allowance and in the garment.

3 Before pulling threads taught, bring the needle at the same angle, catching the loop of the previous stitch.

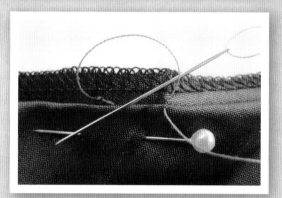

4 Pull gently until the threads lie flat but do not pucker the hem, as shown. Move across approximately ⅜in (1cm) to the right and repeat the actions.

5 This stitch is virtually invisible and, because no threads are left exposed on the inside, it is also strong.

1

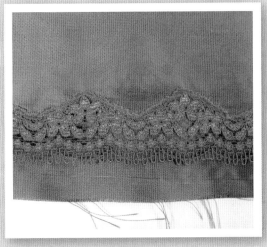

2

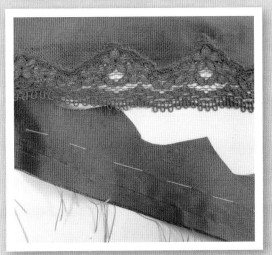

3

Lace-bordered hem

Often used as a way to edge lingerie, this hem is equally gorgeous for a bridal gown, or even to edge the lining as a cheeky little surprise!

1 Place your lace trim so that the bottom edge lays along the desired hem length and pin it into position.

2 If stitching by hand, sew tiny stitches along the upper edge of the lace, working from the right side of the fabric so you can see the finished effect. If by machine, as shown, set your machine to a short, narrow zigzag and, using invisible thread, follow the upper edge of the lace.

3 Trim any excess fabric away from behind the lace, leaving just a few millimetres of fabric.

BIAS- OR RIBBON-BOUND HEM

This hem is used in bridal wear, most often as a decorative finish for tulle or netting (see page 54 for more detailed instruction).

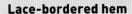

Crin

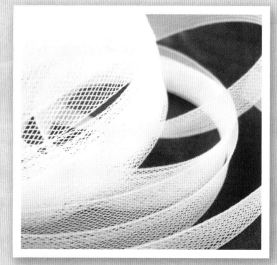

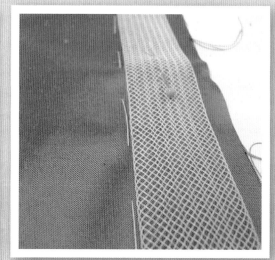

Bagged out with crin or horsehair braid

When a skirt is very full at the hem, or made from crisp fabric, this gives a bit of extra body and helps the fabric to fall in large luxurious folds.

1 For this to work, the skirt and lining must be the same length; trim hem as required. Tack along the desired hem line all the way around the skirt. On the inside of the fabric, lay the crin (also known as a horsehair braid) in the hem allowance, flush with the tack line, and pin into position, as shown. Stitch with a straight stitch ¼in (5mm) down the centre of the crin.

2 With the right side of fabric facing the right side of the lining, matching the seams, jut the lining ⅝in (1.5cm) beyond the fabric edge then pin through the existing stitch line.

3 Stitch over the first row of stitching, then turn the skirts right way out and press the hem, pulling the outer fabric taught round the edge of the crin to create a crisp hemline.

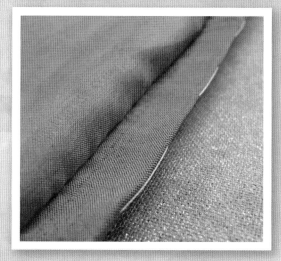

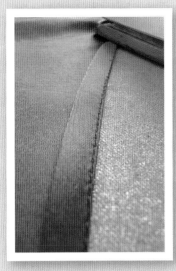

1

2

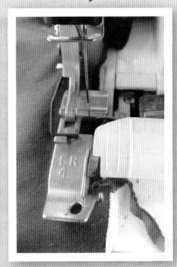

3

Satin-stitch hem

A decorative machine finish that can either match or contrast with the fabric. Perfect for hemming lightweight satins and sheer fabrics. This type of hem can be worked with either a sewing machine or an overlocker.

On the sewing machine

1 Sew a straight line of stitching at the desired finished hemline, then press the hem allowance to the inside along this line.

2 Set the machine to a very short zigzag of medium width. Line up the fabric so that the needle lands either side of the straight stitch, falling just off the pressed edge when swinging to the right. Stitch around the entire hem in this manner then trim away the excess fabric as close as you can to the zigzag without snipping the stitching.

On the overlocker

3 Set the machine to use three threads (of a suitable quality, see page 36). Adjust the settings to a short, narrow stitch and remove the stitching finger. Trim the hem allowance so that it's parallel to the desired hemline all the way round. (Depending on your confidence in your cutting skills and in using the overlocker, the trimmed allowance could be ⅜in (1cm), then use the excess to practise the stitch.) Once completely happy with the settings, overlock along the hemline.

Useful Tip

If you are using a very gauzy fabric and cannot get a good effect using satin stitch on the overlocker, trim the hem allowance to a skimpy ¼in (5mm), then drop the blade and stitch along the hemline. The stitch will be forming around a greater number of fibres and should be more secure.

Hand Sewing

There is an intimate connection that you have with a garment when you've lavished it with the attention that comes with hand sewing, and when could this be more important than with your own wedding dress? Don't forget it's the little touches that set a handmade dress apart from a shop-bought garment.

Threading a needle

To thread a needle for hand sewing, take a long piece of thread then pass both ends through the eye, keeping the cut ends shorter than the loop. Make a tiny stitch on the fabric to be stitched and pass the needle through the loop. Hey presto – a knotless thread, ready to sew!

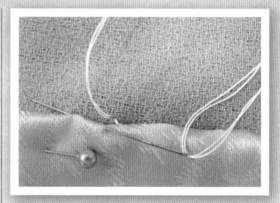

Tacking or basting

This is a temporary stitch commonly used for seams before machine stitching. It is the simplest of all stitches and is achieved by using a single thread with a knot at the end. To ensure ease of removal, tacking is often sewn in a contrasting thread so it can be seen easily. Pass the needle in and out of the fabric at regular intervals between ¼in (5mm) and ⅝in (1.5cm) apart – if tacking a seam before machine stitching, be sure to stitch ⅛in (2–3mm) in from the finished seam line so that the tacking thread does not get caught in the machine stitching.

Slip stitch

This is a durable and almost invisible method of attaching a finished or folded edge to another layer of fabric, such as attaching lining to the inside of a zip, joining the bodice and skirt linings at a waist seam, or catching down a bias binding where machine topstitching looks too commercial. This stitch takes a bit of practice to get a fast, even rhythm, but you'll use it a lot in finely finished clothing so it's worth persevering!

Work from left to right, needle pointing left. Secure the thread, then make a stitch approximately ¼in (5mm) long, passing through the folded edge. Emerge from the fold and catch the adjacent fabric with a tiny stitch. Repeat this stitch, keeping the visible stitches tiny.

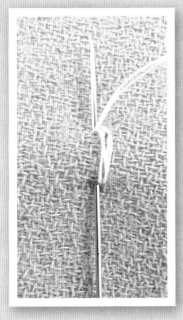

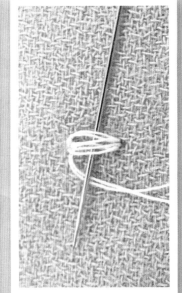

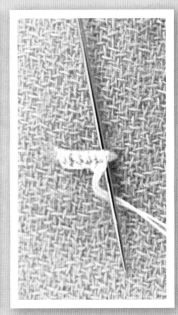

1   **2a**   **2b**

Worked loop

There are times that a button closure is the most attractive, but neither a buttonhole nor a rouleau loop is suitable, especially when working with sheer or fine fabrics. A worked loop can be used as a delicate alternative to a buttonhole or as the eye for a hook and eye closure.

1 Mark the fabric where the button loop is to be sewn, with two marks wide enough to span the hook. Using double thread for strength, secure the thread to the fabric. Make several even stitches directly on top of one another, spanning your two marks, taking care not to pucker the fabric. Secure the last stitch with a tiny backstitch.

2 Work from left to right with the point of the needle towards your body. Pass the needle below the threads, keeping the previous stitch beneath the needle's point. A decorative stitch will form, wrapped around the threads (**2a**). Repeat this until you have covered the entire length of the threads (**2b**), then take the needle to the back of the fabric and finish the thread with tiny backstitches. To make a worked loop suitable for fastening a button, just make the stitches spanning the two marks slightly loose so they form an arc, test to check the button fits, then continue as described above.

1

2a

2b

Attaching beads and sequins

Stabilize the area designated for embellishment. For opaque fabrics, a piece of either iron-on or stitch-in interfacing (see page 29) applied to the back will give sufficient support. For sheer fabrics, tack a piece of tissue or tear away interfacing that can later be removed. Then draw the design lightly onto the surface using a fade-away marker.

1 Once the thread is secured, beads and sequins can be threaded into the needle and attached to the fabric using short stitches, as shown. Travel between beads on the back of the fabric but do not attempt to carry the thread more than ¾in (2cm). Instead, secure the thread, snip and start again. Heavy beads should be anchored after each bead with a tiny stitch on the back of the fabric – this way, if the thread gets caught you should not lose an entire run of beads.

2 There are many combinations of beads and sequins, attached in a single stitch that create texture and variation in a design and, once combined, these can make beautiful motifs (**2a** & **2b**).

Useful Tip

Use a beading needle to sew your decoration and, if you can manage to thread the very fine needle, a double thread (see page 62). Regular thread is easiest to manage, but if you are sewing translucent crystals or sewing onto sheer fabrics, invisible thread will look best.

Darts

Darts allow shaping in a garment when you don't want to use an entire seam.
They are perfect for removing excess fabric at the waist, shoulder or bust.
There are two types of dart – single point or double point.

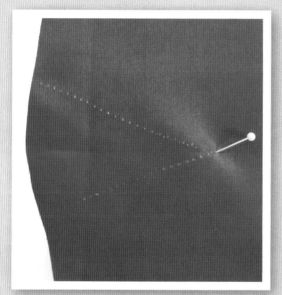

1a

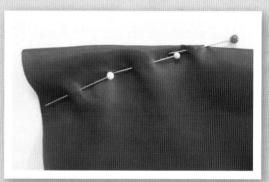

1b

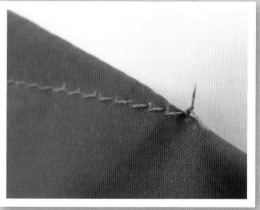

2

Single point dart

This dart has a single point (where the stitching tapers off the fabric) and the other end of the dart will disappear into a seam or off the edge of the garment into the waistband or hem.

1 Transfer your pattern markings onto the fabric using chalk, carbon paper and a tracing wheel or a fade-away marker. Stab a pin into the point of the dart (**1a**) then pinch the fabric from the blunt end towards the dart point, matching the stitching lines. Pin together (**1b**).

2 Starting from the blunt end, stitch the dart (use a backstitch at the beginning). To finish the point, if the fabric is thick, you can backstitch and then cut the threads short. If the fabric is very fine or sheer, this method may cause the fabric to pucker, so leave the threads long and either tie them off or hand sew the ends.

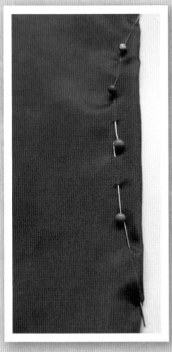

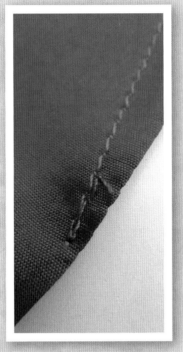

1

2

3

Double point dart

This dart has two tapered ends and is most often used to nip in the waist of a dress, jacket or blouse to create a smooth silhouette.

1 Transfer your pattern markings onto the fabric. Stab pins into the disappearing point of both ends. With right sides together, match the stitching line and pin the dart.

2 If your fabric is thick you can stitch from one end of the dart to the other, backstitching at both ends to secure.

3 For light fabrics, start stitching the dart from the centre towards the point, finishing the dart end by hand. Repeat this process to complete the other end of the dart, as shown. For sheer fabrics, start at one point with no backstitch and continue to the other point and tie or hand sew the ends to finish.

Useful Tip

To transfer markings that fall in the middle of a pattern piece (when carbon paper is not suitable), stab a long pin straight through the paper and layers of fabric. Carefully mark all the layers of fabric at the point the pin penetrates.

Boning

Historically the 'bones' in a garment were made of wood, ivory, or whalebone. Nowadays, lighter weight and more flexible boning gives a garment a smooth appearance and reinforcement – it also improves posture.

Plastic boning

Plastic boning is easily cut with craft scissors and is flexible, versatile and lightweight – ideal for stiffening bodices, collars and hooped skirts. It does not recover well once kinked, however, so may not stand up to the rigours of a tight-fitting bodice or corset. For a wedding dress, it is perhaps best used in conjunction with spiral boning. It is brilliant for stiffening the centre of bodice panels as it can be applied directly to the interlining (see page 29) without causing too much bulk.

Plastic boning must be cut shorter than the panel to which it is attached – ¼in (5mm) inside the top and bottom seam lines – so that once sewn, it doesn't interfere with the seam. The ends of the cut boning must sealed or it can easily penetrate the garment's fibres and become extremely uncomfortable. I tend to melt these ends by holding the cut end ⅜in (1cm) above a naked flame; allow the plastic to soften and gloop into a soft blob.

1 Cut a small, square scrap of your bodice fabric and fold it over the cut end of your boning – this will prevent the end from poking through the finished garment. If attaching the boning to a foundation bodice or lining, then it is fine for the stitching to show all the way through.

2 Set your machine stitch to a wide zigzag then stitch through the boning, joining it to the fabric beneath and taking care to catch the fabric tabs top and bottom.

Plastic boning

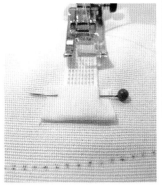

1

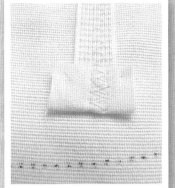

2

Spiral boning

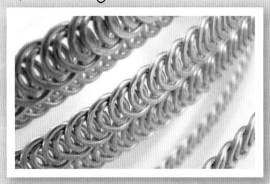

Spiral boning

This heavy duty, highly flexible boning is more expensive and heavier than plastic but doesn't kink, which works particularly well for very curvy girls. To cut spiral boning you will need a sturdy pair of edge pliers, and to finish the ends with end caps you'll need one (or two) pairs of small long-nose pliers.

1 Mark the spiral across where it is to be cut, and cut the outer wire on each side (**1a**). The spiral is constructed of two springs that are crushed together, therefore snipping one wire at each side will cut through the entire structure. Do not try to cut the entire width – it will really hurt your hands and is unnecessary. To finish the ends, pop the raw end of the spiral into the end cap and carefully squash the cap with small pliers until it grips into the spiral, taking care not to create any sharp edges (**1b & 1c**).

2 Spiral boning must be inserted into a channel, as it cannot be stitched directly to a fabric. You can use either a tightly woven cotton or polyester tape or a bias binding as a boning channel. Pin the tape onto the interlining panel, tucking the top end under by ⅜in (1cm) and leaving the bottom to extend to the bottom edge of the panel.

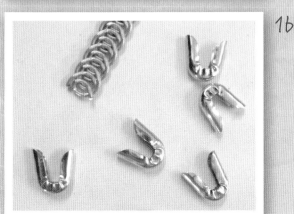

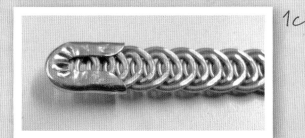

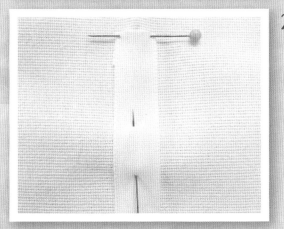

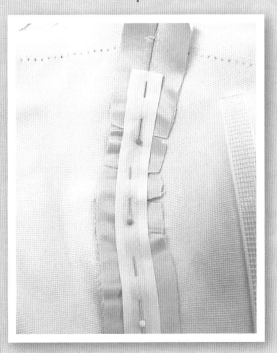

3 Stitch all the way around the edge of the tape, leaving the bottom end open to insert the boning, as shown. Slide the boning into the channel and stitch across just below the boning to hold it tightly into the channel. The boning should end at least ¼in (5mm) above the seam line at the lower edge.

4 These channels can also be sewn onto a seam, which is especially useful to get a formed curve over the bust, and to stop the side seams from kinking. Prepare the seam by pressing open and clipping into curves if necessary – just don't trim seam allowances. Cut a length of tape ⅜in (1cm) shorter than the seam – at the top edge, tuck the end under so that the end is ¼in (5mm) below the seam line. The fold will stop the boning from popping out at the top. Pin the tape directly down the centre of the seam, stabbing the pins through the seam line.

5 Flip the garment out of the way so that you can sew the edge of the tape onto the seam allowance without catching the garment. Repeat down the other side of seam allowance, as shown. It may be necessary to catch the top edge to the seam allowance by hand. Insert the boning and firmly stitch across the bottom to prevent it escaping.

Fastenings

Essential to the finish of a garment, fastenings can be decorative or virtually invisible. Think about the practicalities of getting into (and out of) your dress, and who you will have to help you on the day.

Buttons

There are two main types of button. Shanked buttons have loops (shanks) on the back that stand proud of the fabric once stitched in. Sew-through buttons have holes through which the thread passes. When sewn flat, sew-through buttons can be used for lightweight fabrics.

Most bridal buttons are either decorative crystal or pearl ball shanked buttons, or self-covered fabric buttons that can easily be made at home from a kit.

Sewing a button

To sew on a single button, use a length of thread approximately 14in (35cm) long. Thread both ends through the needle, leaving the loop end longer. Make a tiny stitch where the button is to be placed, then thread the needle through the loop made by the stitch. Now you have a firmly attached double thread with no knot. Sew the button on, keeping all stitches in the same spot.

Making a thread shank

To use a sew-through button with rouleau loops or on thick fabrics you'll need to make a thread shank. To do this, lay a matchstick across the face of the button, bring stitches up through one of the holes in the button, over the matchstick and back down through the other hole. Once you've done enough stitches (five or six), with the needle and thread between the fabric and the back of button, remove the matchstick then wind the thread firmly around the stitches to form a shank. Fasten the ends by stitching through the shank.

Attaching a button to lace

If sewing a button onto lace it is advisable to use a tiny reinforcing button or small doubled square of fabric to the back of the fabric to keep the outer fabric from being torn. When attaching the button, pass the needle through both the fabric and this reinforcement with each stitch.

Useful Tip

Unless buttons are purely decorative or less than 1¼in (3cm) apart, a new piece of thread should be used for each one.

Rouleau

Rouleau is very versatile – once you have got to grips with the technique you can make spaghetti straps, lacing, button loops or even Chinese knot-work frogging... Keep in mind though that the width and thickness of your initial strip of fabric will determine its chunkiness, so experiment first. Here, I have used a heavyweight crêpe with approximately ¾in (2cm) wide strips.

1 Lay out your fabric, then mark and cut the true bias strips from your fabric. To join strips of bias fabric together, see page 54.

2 With right sides together, fold the strips in half lengthwise and pin together, as shown. Using the edge of your machine foot as a guide, stitch down the full length, approximately ¼in (5mm) from the folded edge. Do not trim the seam allowances.

3 Thread your rouleau hook (see page 38) – hook end first – into the tube and hook around a small amount of the fabric at the other end. Make sure the latch closes properly, otherwise you'll come unthreaded.

4 Gently pull the hooked end back into the tube (keeping the tension on the hook so it doesn't come unlatched). Ease the fabric along until the rouleau is turned right side out.

1

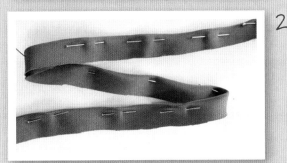

2

3

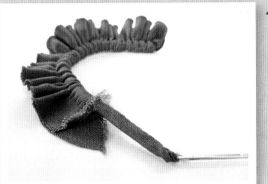

4

5 If using rouleau as loops for buttons, make paper templates for the placement of your buttons and/or loops. Once happy with the spacing, transfer the marking in the seam allowance on the right side of your fabric. To make button loops, measure the circumference of your buttons and add 1¼in (3cm) – this is the length of rouleau you need to cut for each loop. Cut a length for each button. If the loops are to carry lacing, make sure to cut enough to pair up either side.

6 Pin the rouleau loops with the raw ends flush to the cut edge of the seam allowance. Stitch along the seam line to secure the loops in place.

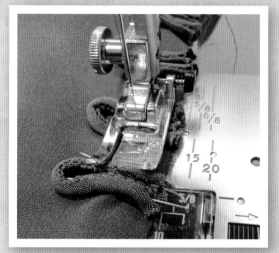

7 Pin the facing or lining of the garment right sides together, with the lining facing down, as shown. At this stage, the loops will be sandwiched between the outer and lining fabric. Stitch over the existing seam line to conceal the previous stitching.

Open out the seam, press seam allowances and the stubby ends of the rouleau towards facing, leaving the outer layer free.

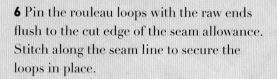

Useful Tip

Pins can be hard to manage, as the rouleau loops can be bulky and tend to roll as they go under the machine foot. Instead, use clear sticky tape – you can stitch right through it.

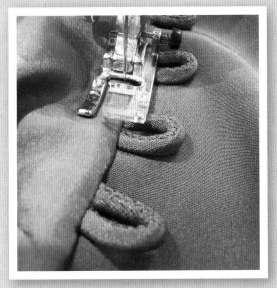

8 Understitch (see page 50) close to the seam line through all layers on the facing side of the seam.

9 Fold facing to inside and press the finished seam edge. The loops will be extended beyond the garment edge.

Poppers, hooks and eyes

Hooks and eyes are best used when they are under a small amount of tension, for example at the top of a zip. Poppers are often used in conjunction with hooks, when fastening a detachable item such as the cap sleeves for 'Florence' (see page 154), or the train on 'Celeste' (see page 122). They hold the openings together and remain fast even when there is no tension and the hooks could otherwise come undone.

To attach either hooks and eyes or poppers, simply stitch by hand, using a double thread (see page 70), passing the needle through the hole in the fastening and into the fabric, using small stitches. Repeat two or three times through each hole, securing threads with a couple of backstitches. As a general rule, the male half of the fastening goes on top.

Hook-and-eye tape

This is a strong fastening technique, and quicker to apply than sewing hooks and eyes individually. The closures rely on being under an even amount of tension to work effectively. I have used hook-and-eye tape for the foundation bodice inside 'Celeste' (see page 109 for instructions).

Hook-and-eye tape

Zips

As long as you have the correct foot for your sewing machine, zips are actually very easy to put in. Two types of foot are best: the traditional zipper foot (**A**) or an invisible zipper foot (also called a cording/pin tucking foot), which has grooves on the bottom (**B**). For bridal wear, the invisible zip is by far the most attractive.

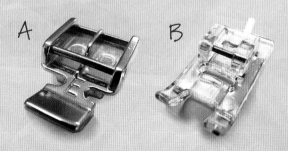

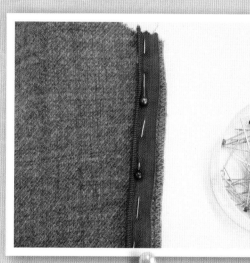

1 Prepare the fabric with 1in (2.5cm) wide strips of interfacing (see page 29) either side of the opening, on the wrong side of the fabric, extending the interfacing 1in (2.5cm) beyond the zip's length.

2 Place the zip right side down onto the right side of the fabric at the seam opening. Keep the top edge of the zip tape flush with the edge of the fabric. Open the zip and pin it to the seam allowance, teeth facing towards the garment.

Useful Tip

If you are inserting the zip across seams (for example, a waist seam), once the first side is sewn, do the zip up and mark onto the zip tape where the seam meets the opposite side of the zip. Match this point on the zip to the seam line on the second side of the opening for perfectly matched seams.

3 Using the invisible zipper foot, line up the needle with the groove just behind the zip teeth – the teeth will roll over slightly as you sew. Sew to within 1in (2.5cm) of the bottom end of the zip teeth.

4 Do the zip up (to stop it twisting) and pin the other side onto the seam allowance as before, unzipping as you go.

Repeat the stitching process down the opposite side (if using a normal zipper foot, you may need to adjust it, or your needle position – follow the guidelines for your machine).

5 Do the zip up and turn the fabrics so that right sides are facing. Pin the seam from the bottom of the zip down towards the hem. Gently swing the end of the zip out of the way so as not to catch it into the seam. Use a traditional zipper foot to stitch from the bottom of the zip stitch line down the seam.

6 Press the seam open and admire your invisible zip.

Useful Tip

Completing the seam after a zip is inserted helps to eliminate puckering at the base of the zip.

Corsages

A beautiful corsage could add the finishing touch to your wedding dress. For a simple rosebud you can use almost any fabric, and for the petals you can use up scraps of crisp (natural fibre) fabrics. For a delicate effect, cut your petals from a mixture of opaque and sheer fabrics, graduating from opaque smaller petals to translucent larger petals.

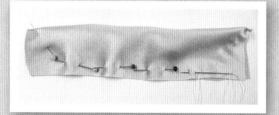

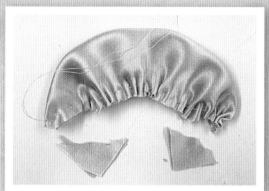

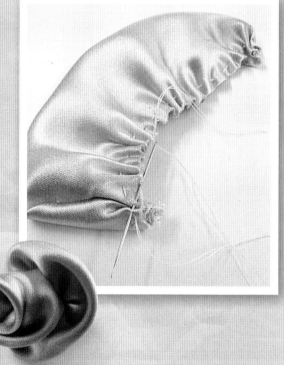

Rosebud

1 To make a rosebud, use a bias strip of fabric – mine was 3 x 6in (7.5 x 15cm). Fold the fabric right sides out, into a long narrow strip, then, using a short tacking stitch (see page 62), sew from the folded edge, curving across to the raw edge, along the length and then curve back to the folded edge.

2 Pull the thread to gather the fabric slightly. Trim the raw edge level beneath the gathering (**2a**). Prepare a needle with double thread (see page 70). Starting from one end, tightly roll the gathered edge of the fabric, keeping the raw edges flush, and stitching in place as you go (**2b**).

You can leave your rose as just a bud, as shown, perhaps clustering several together to create a larger corsage.

1

2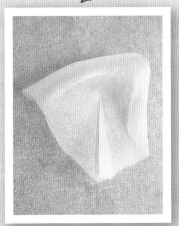

3a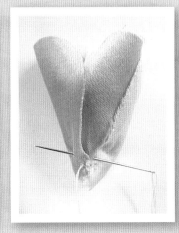

3b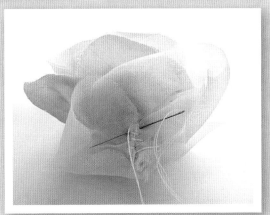

Full rose

For a full rose, cut petals using the templates provided on pattern sheet C. You will need 5 small petals, 6 medium and 7 large.

1 Dampen the petals with water to make them pliable. Roll the individual petals around a pencil or knitting needle, then leave them somewhere warm until they are completely dry before sliding them off the mould. The smallest petals should be rolled from side to side, the medium petals from top to bottom, and the largest petals should be rolled into a cone, with the pointed end starting in the dimple at the top of the petal.

2 Once dry, for the largest petals make a pleat in the bottom edge on the petal and use the tip of an iron to press the crease in.

3 To assemble, add petals one at a time, stitching them to the base of the rosebud (**3a**), turning the flower as you add each petal so that they overlap. As the petals get larger you may need to add a few extra stitches to the

sides of each petal to hold the shape (**3b**). Although you will be sewing from the back, keep turning the corsage over and checking how it looks from the front. If you are using a mix of fabrics, check they are evenly distributed rather than clumped together.

Once all the petals are sewn on you can attach a hair slide or brooch back, or stitch your corsage directly onto your dress. Why not cluster several flowers of different sizes together?

Net Underskirts

A net underskirt can dramatically alter the silhouette of a garment. It will add bounce and flirtiness to shorter dresses and ballgown glamour to full-length styles. By varying the lengths of tiers and the number of layers, you can create everything from just a little fullness to a full-blown fairytale princess dress.

Underskirt basics

Just two basic methods are needed to create a multitude of silhouettes: circles and tiers. Decide on the shape you want, then build it up gradually, layering the net until you achieve the silhouette you desire.

BELOW ARE THREE UNDERSKIRT STYLES AND THEIR NETTING COMPONENTS.

A

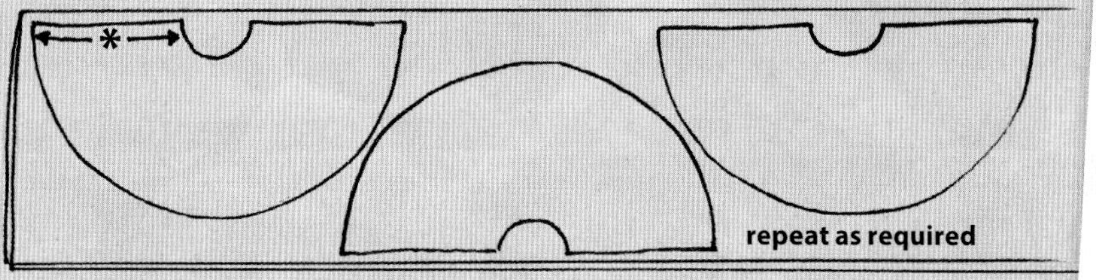

repeat as required

✳ = hipbone to hem

B

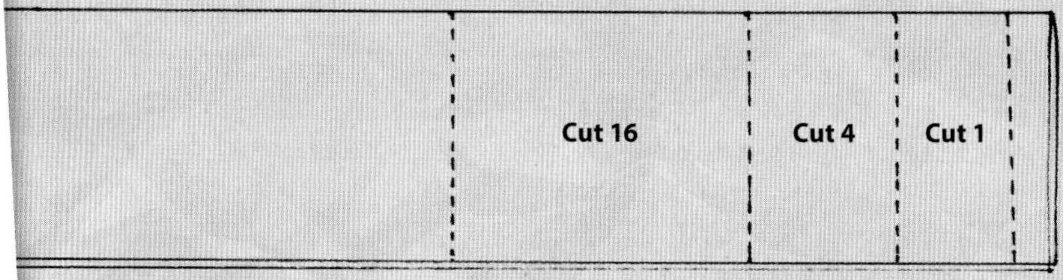

Cut 16   Cut 4   Cut 1

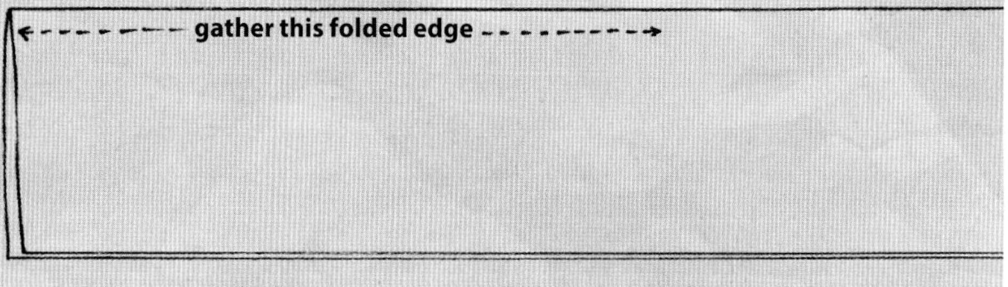

gather this folded edge

C

Freestanding Petticoat

This underskirt has three components: a yoke, layers of netting and a lining. The outer layer is made with semicircles of net, seamed and gathered onto the yoke. The underlayer of net is made of tiers gathered on a ratio of 4:1 (this ratio makes construction easy as the fabric can be simply folded to find quarter points, avoiding the need for complicated measurements). As wearing netting next to the skin, or directly over hosiery, can be uncomfortable, prickly and itchy, the bottom layer is made in lining fabric. For the petticoat shown, you will need about 11yd (10m) of dress net.

Yoke and lining

1 For the yoke, cut a rectangle of lining fabric 6in (15cm) longer than your Lower Hip (LH) measurement and 3in (7.5cm) deeper than your Waist to Lower Hip (WLH) measurement. Stitch the rectangle together along the shorter sides to create a shallow tube. Finish seam allowances.

Make a channel for the elastic (using a non-roll elastic of at least 1in (2.5cm) width will be the most comfortable). Fold over the top edge of the tube by ⅜in (1cm), press, then fold over again, this time ⅜in (1cm) wider than the width of your elastic. Press and pin both edges of this channel, as shown.

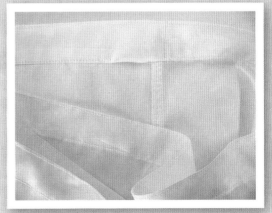

1

2 Stitch close to the upper edge of the fold, parallel to the edge of the fabric all the way around, then stitch along the pinned line, leaving a gap of 2in (5cm) for threading your elastic through the waist channel later.

2

3

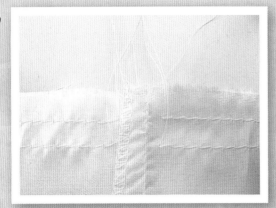

4

GATHERING

This is an essential technique used to fit a larger length of fabric into a smaller space. It can be used to ease in a sleeve (as on page 159), create fullness in a skirt (as on these pages) or create ruffles or ruching (as on page 115). The greater the amount of fabric and the smaller the space, the fuller or puffier the effect.

Stitch two rows of long straight stitch, one at ⅜in (1cm) from the edge and one at ³⁄₁₆in (2cm). Do not backstitch at the start or finish, and leave the threads long at each end (see photo 3).

At one end of the stitching, pull all the threads to the surface and tie them together securely. (This will stop them from being pulled out when we gather the fabric.) From the other end, gently pull the two threads on the upper surface of the fabric, taking care not to pull the ones on the back (see photo 5).

Slide the fullness in the fabric along the threads until the gathered piece sits flat in place. Spread the fabric evenly, to create uniform gathers, and pin in place, pinning crossways (as in photo 6).

To secure the gathers, stitch directly down the middle of the two rows of gathering threads at ⅝in (1.5cm) seam allowance, either sewing into a seam or securing with bias binding, as required for your garment. Once finished, remove the gathering threads.

3 For the lining, cut two panels of lining fabric, using the full width from selvedge to selvedge (this will vary in width but doesn't matter) and 1in (2.5cm) longer than your LH to hem measurement. With right sides facing, pin and stitch the two panels together along the selvedges, to form a wide tube.

Divide one of the raw edges into quarters (this will help you when attaching the lining to the yoke) and mark these points. Prepare this edge with two rows of gathering threads (see 'Gathering', right).

4 Now divide the lower edge of the yoke into quarters and mark these points. With right sides facing, match up the markings on the yoke to the markings on the lining.

5

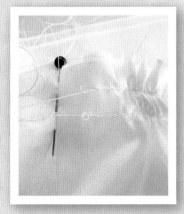

6

7

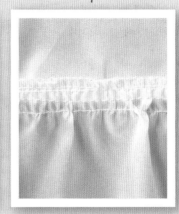

8

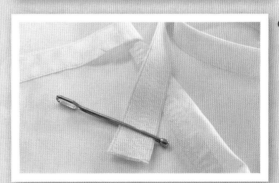

9

10

5 Pull up the gathering threads at the top of the lining, easing the fullness until the fabric fits perfectly to the yoke.

6 With right sides together, gathers even and pins crossways, stitch directly down the centre of the gathering threads at ⅝in (1.5cm) seam allowance.

7 Finish the seam (overlocking or zig-zagging work best) and press upwards.

8 Hem the lower edge by turning the raw edge over by ⅝in (1.5cm) twice and stitching close to the turned edge (see page 56 for hem techniques). Press. You now have a blank canvas on which to build your petticoat.

9 Using a bodkin/split pin, thread the elastic into the hole you left in the elastic casing, being careful not to twist the elastic.

10 Try the petticoat on and adjust the elastic until comfortable (usually it will be a couple of inches shorter than your own waist measurement). Pin the elastic securely with an overlap of 1in (2.5cm), and zigzag stitch across the join to secure. Allow the sewn elastic to 'ping' inside the opening then stitch up the opening with a straight stitch.

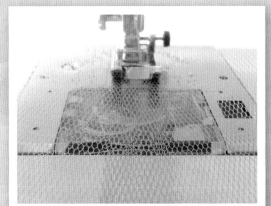

12

Netting tiers

11 Join panels of net by overlapping the seam allowances by approximately ⅝in (1.5cm) and stitching down the centre.

12 Gather the upper edge of each tier by running two rows of stitching at ⅜in (1cm) and ¾in (2cm) from the upper edge as described in making the petticoat lining.

13 Join tiers of net by overlapping the gathered edge of the net over the flat edge of the tier above and sew together using a regular length stitch, as shown. Attach the net layers onto the basic petticoat base above the seam line on the lining.

Useful Tip

Do not try to gather too much fabric in one go. It is better to make a break in the stitching and gather in sections no greater than four widths of net at a time. Otherwise you will put too much strain on the threads, causing them to snap.

14

14 To attach bias binding to netting, fold the binding in half along its length and press, keeping the edges flush. Slot the netting into the groove and stitch along the edge closest to the net.

15 When you get back to the beginning, tuck the ends inside and overlap the binding to create a neat finish (**15a** & **15b**).

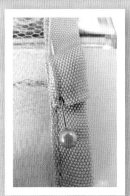

15a   15b

Your finished petticoat is ready to rock!

Finishing the hem

If your petticoat will show at the hem of your dress, it is really nice to give it a beautifully finished edge. Bias binding, ribbon or lace edging or satin stitch are all attractive (see pages 56–61). Using a binding can be time consuming, although simple enough to do. You can purchase decorative bias binding from good haberdashers or make your own (see page 54).

'What a woman wears on her wedding day isn't "just a frock" – it is the essence of the day.'

CAROLINE CASTIGLIANO, DESIGNER

Amélie

This is the
perfect chance to
add a little colour
to your wedding outfit.
A flash of petticoat and a
floral corsage set off the blossom
weave of this adorable taffeta dress.

Amélie

This fabulous fifties-style dress is perfect for first-time stitchers, as it uses the basic bodice pattern with just minor adjustments and a little added ease for comfort. The pattern pieces for the full skirts are easy to draw and look fabulous in crisp fabrics such as dupion, taffeta and duchesse satin, especially when teamed up with a flirty net petticoat. This is a great style for those with fabulous legs or a shoe fetish – show off perfect pins and statement shoes in this tea-length gown.

Drawing the Pattern

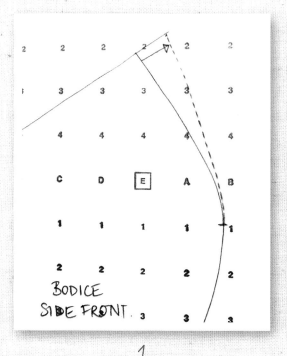

1

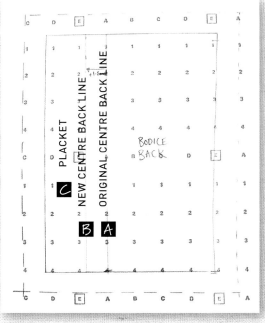

2

Bodice pattern

1 Using your personalized bodice pattern (see 'How to Use the Patterns', page 42), trace all the bodice pieces down to the waist, without seam allowances. Now draw a straight line across the waistline, leaving a space of at least 1in (2.5cm) around the edge of each pattern piece for your adjustments. Draw a Centre-Back (CB) panel for each of the left and right sides, in mirror image.

For the side front panel, add ¾in (2cm) at the top of the front edge, tapering to bust point, as shown (the side back panel remains unaltered).

2 For the CB bodice panel, add ⅝in (1.5cm) to the entire length from the original CB line (**A**) to create a new CB line (**B**), and then, only on the right-hand side panel, add a further 1¼in (3cm) onto the left CB edge as a placket (**C**), as shown. The Centre-Front (CF) bodice panel and the side back panels remain unaltered.

Measure the new waistline of your bodice pattern (remembering to include both sides of the bodice) – we'll refer to this measurement as 'X' (it should be approximately 1¼in/3cm larger than your actual waist measurement).

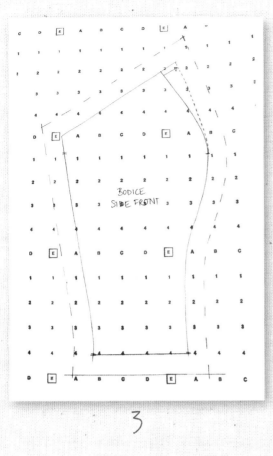

BODICE
SIDE FRONT

3

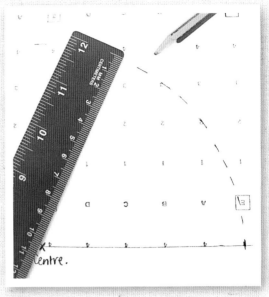

4

X
centre.

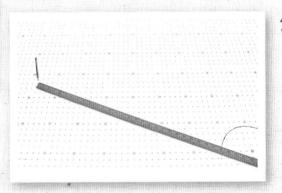

5

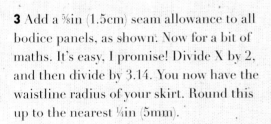

3 Add a ⅝in (1.5cm) seam allowance to all bodice panels, as shown. Now for a bit of maths. It's easy, I promise! Divide X by 2, and then divide by 3.14. You now have the waistline radius of your skirt. Round this up to the nearest ¼in (5mm).

Skirt pattern

4 For the skirt pattern, draw a long straight line parallel to the edge (leaving enough space to add the seam allowance), ⅝in (1.5cm) along one side of a large piece of pattern paper. Mark a point on this line, near one end – this is called centre point. From your centre point, mark your radius measurement from

Step 3 along the line. Using a tape measure or ruler to get an accurate measurement, draw a semi-circle round this centre point, using the radius measurement, as shown. This line will be the waistline of your skirt.

5 Add the radius measurement to your desired skirt length and draw a new, much larger semi-circle from the same centre point to mark the finished hemline of your dress, as shown. You will need a complete semi-circle for the front of your skirt and two quarter-circles for the back of your skirt.

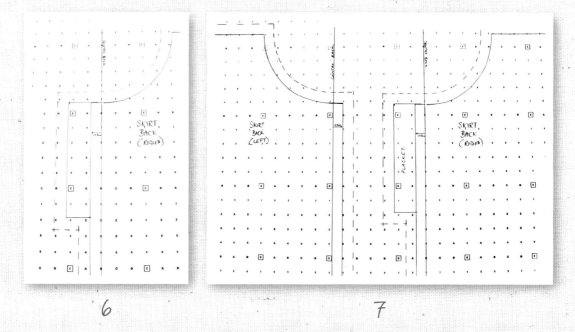

6

7

6 The Centre Backs (CB) of the two skirt panels need to be treated individually, as with the bodice pattern, so for these, add ⅝in (1.5cm) to the CB edge of both pieces – this is the new CB line. On the right back panel, add a placket, 1¼in (3cm) wide and 6¼in (16cm) long.

7 Add ⅝in (1.5cm) seam allowance to all edges of the skirt patterns, as shown, and add 1¼in (3cm) hem allowance to the hem.

Upper bodice pattern

For the upper bodice you will need your Across Front (AF), Across Back (AB), Bust Front (BF) and Bust Back (BB) measurements. Select the front panel piece according to your BF measurement (see page 40) and the back panel according to your BB measurement. Then, using the technique

shown on page 43 to tweak the pattern, draw a new line wherever necessary so that the pattern matches your measurements. To lengthen or shorten the upper bodice pattern, follow the guidelines on page 43. Your new Nape to Waist (NW) measurement should be equal to the sum of the CB edges of the bodice and upper bodice. Add ⅝in (1.5cm) seam allowance to all edges.

Making the toile

Using your personalized patterns, make a toile for your dress, using calico for the main bodice and skirt, and muslin or similar fine fabric for the upper bodice. For detailed instructions on how to do this, see page 44. Try the toile on, make any adjustments as necessary and transfer the alterations to your pattern pieces. You are now ready to make your wedding gown.

Making the Dress

Once you have a fitting pattern, we are ready to cut the fabrics. You should have:

- personalized bodice pattern (with any toile alterations) – for main dress fabric, lining and interlining
- upper bodice pattern – for chiffon, organza or georgette
- skirt pattern – for dress fabric and lining.

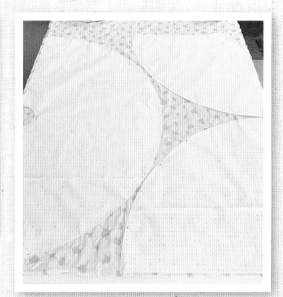

The layout of your pattern will vary depending on your personal measurements and the width of your fabric, but you must adhere to the grainline when laying your pattern out.

1 The side seams of the skirt panels will be parallel to the selvedge of your fabric, so that the straight grain runs from side to side. As we have drawn a piece for each panel, these pieces will be laid on a single layer of the right side of the fabric.

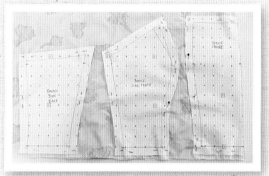

2 The bodice panels can be laid on the wrong side of the folded fabric, with the CF panel flush with the folded edge (**2a**) and the back bodice panels also need to be laid on the single, right side of the fabric (**2b**).

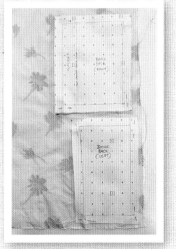

Cut the main bodice and skirt in both the outer fabric and the lining. The upper bodice will likely be in chiffon, organza or georgette, and the main bodice will also have a stable interlining. I have used a stable bleached calico as an interlining to prevent the bodice from having any translucency and to give a little firmness to this close-fitting bodice.

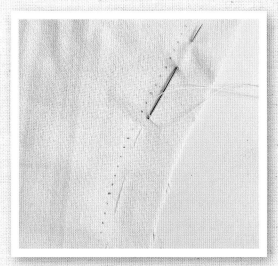

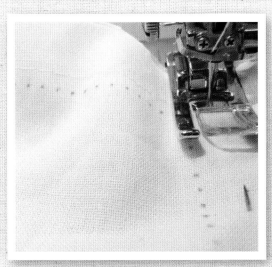

3 Using a tracing wheel and carbon paper, mark the pattern pieces ready for construction by outlining the seam lines and markings on the interlining and lining (the fabric is pinned to the back of the paper) (**3a** & **3b**). No need to mark the outer fabric.

4 Layer up the interlining and the outer fabric, placing each individual piece right side facing of fabric to the table and markings facing up. Pin the pieces together, matching the edges exactly, then mount them, tacking either by hand (**4a**) or using a machine (on the longest straight stitch) (**4b**) within the seam allowance. Take care to keep the layers flat and do not allow wrinkles to creep in at this early stage.

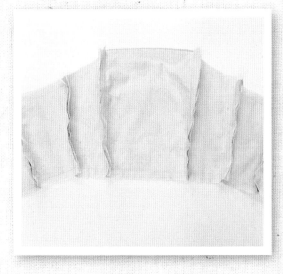

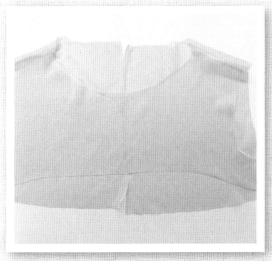

5 Stitch the mounted outer bodice panels together, matching tops and bottoms and any other markings.

6 Clip the seam allowances and press them open, as shown. Stitch the bodice lining together in the same manner, taking care to stitch them together in the mirror image of the bodice outer.

7 Make the upper bodice by joining the pieces together at the side seams and shoulders, using French seams (see page 55).

8 Hem the back edge of the upper bodice by simply turning the seam allowance over twice and topstitching (see page 56) close to the inner folded edge.

9

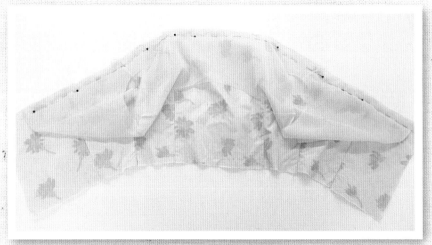

10

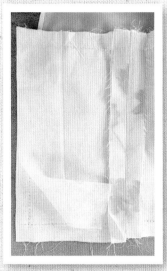

11

12

9 With the right sides of the upper bodice and main bodice facing, match the side seams and CF. The back edge of the upper bodice should be matched exactly to the CB marking. Pin and stitch along the seam line, taking care to keep the seam allowances open when stitching.

10 The bodice will now look like this...

11 You can now make the rouleau (see page 71) for the bodice. Before attaching the rouleau strips, press a strip of interfacing (see page 29) onto the interlining onto both edges, on the inside of the back bodice, roughly 2in (5cm) wide. This reinforces the fabric where the buttons and rouleau are to be attached.

12 Once you have pinned and stitched the rouleau loops, turn the seam allowance to the inside and press, as shown.

13

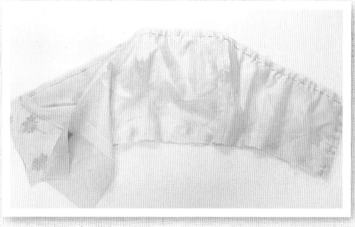

14

15

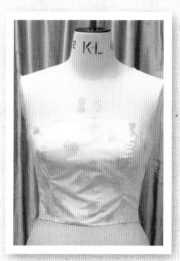

16a

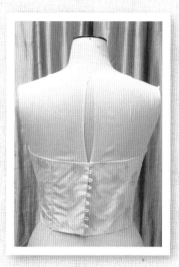

16b

13 If you wish to add a label, attach it to the lining on the left-hand side, sufficiently far in from the edge so as not to get caught in the final stitching.

14 With the right sides together, and the upper bodice tucked down in between and out of the way, line up the raw edges of the outer bodice and bodice lining. Pin and stitch along the top edge and back edges, leaving the waist seam open.

15 Snip the top corners of the bodice away at an angle to reduce bulk.

16 Now turn the bodice right sides out, understitch (see page 50) the lining and press to the inside. Your bodice should look like this (**16a** & **16b**).

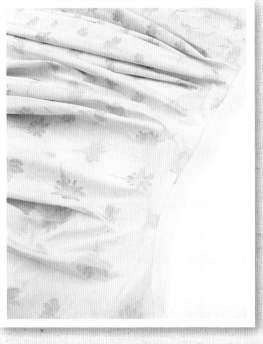

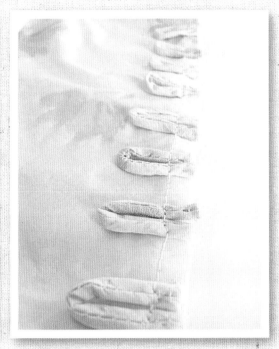

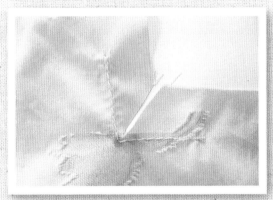

19a

19b

17 To make the skirt, join the outer fabric together at the side seams. Leave the CB seam open at this stage. Repeat this process for the skirt lining, then stitch together in a mirror image of the outer skirt, making sure the plackets match once the wrong sides are facing.

18 Apply interfacing and attach rouleau loops as before onto the left-hand side of the skirt, spacing them evenly to match the loops already attached to the bodice. Extend the loops on the skirt 6in (15cm) from the waistline to correspond with the placket.

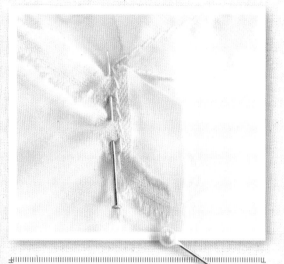

19 On the outer skirt fabric, reinforce the corner at the bottom of the placket on the right-hand side by stitching along the seam line (**19a**), then snip into the corner (**19b**). Repeat this process on the corresponding piece of the skirt lining.

20 Pin and stitch the CB seam of the skirt from the reinforced point down to the hem (**20a** & **20b**). Repeat this process for the skirt lining.

21 Stay stitch (see Glossary, page 170) the skirt's waist seam, stitching just within the seam allowance to prevent the waist from stretching, then tack or baste (see page 62) the skirt onto the bodice at the waist seam. Try the dress, ready to fit the skirt hem.

Useful Tip

Don't worry about trying to understitch right into the corner – just stitch as far as you can.

21

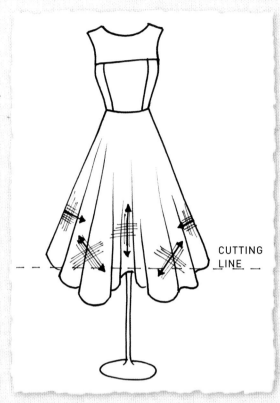

22

CUTTING LINE

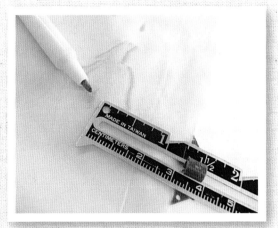

23

22 Due to the skirts being circular, some parts of the hem will be falling on the straight grain and some on the bias of the fabric. The looser the weave of your fabric, the more the hem will dip at the bias sections.

To address this issue, you must put the dress on and get help to trim the hem level. You can either do this by measuring the distance from the floor upwards and making marks on the fabric at the cutting line, as shown, or, if you have access to a hem marker (a stand fitted with a handheld chalk puffer), use this. If your fabric is lightweight and crisp, the hem may already be perfectly level. Repeat this process with the lining to ensure it will not hang down below the skirt.

23 Mark the hemline of the skirt 1¼in (3cm) from the raw edge with either chalk, tacking/basting or a fade-away marker, as shown. Remove the basting/tacking at the waistline to separate the skirt and skirt lining from the bodice. Then follow the instructions on page 60 for a bagged-out hem with a crin or horsehair braid.

Useful Tip

If you are using a floppy fabric, do not attempt to use horsehair braid/crin to finish the hem. Instead, finish the skirt and lining hems separately. Finish the raw edge of the outer skirt then hand lockstitch (see page 58) the hem turning. Check the lining doesn't droop below the outer skirt, then turn the allowance and machine hem.

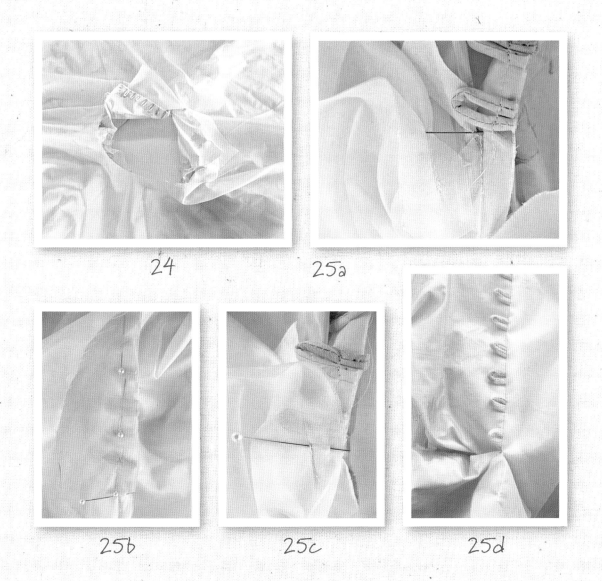

24

25a

25b

25c

25d

24 Turn the skirt right sides out, enclosing the raw hem edges as shown, and finish the back openings of the skirt, one side of the CB seam at a time.

25 Now this part could seem tricky, but it sounds harder than it is. Twisting the fabric so that right sides are facing, match the reinforced corners of lining and skirt outer on the left-hand side (**25a**), then pin and stitch from exactly the point of the reinforced corner up towards the waist edge (**25b**), encasing the raw ends of the rouleau loops (**25c**). Once turned the right side out, it will look like this (**25d**).

26d

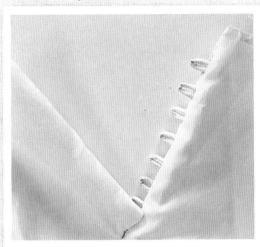

26c

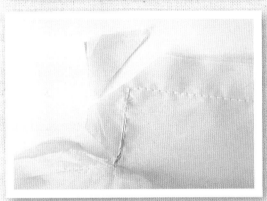

26 Again, twisting the fabrics so that the right sides are facing, match the right-hand side of the skirt opening, starting from the same reinforced corner point and, matching the raw edges of the placket, pin around the right-angled seam of the placket (**26a**) then stitch this seam (**26b**) before trimming off the excess fabric on the corner (**26c**). Turn the edges right sides out and press firmly (**26d**).

27 Smooth the skirt layers together, matching the raw edges at the waist, then pin and stitch through both layers, along the existing stay-stitch line.

27

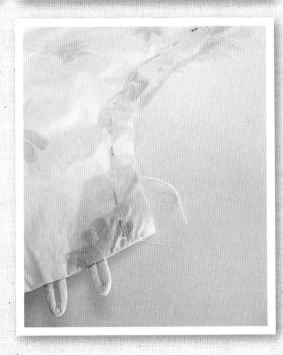

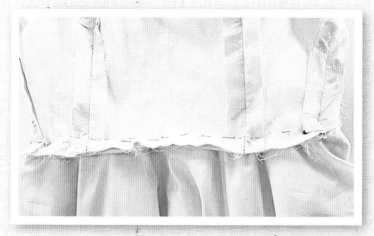

28 With right sides together, matching CB and side seams, pin and then stitch the bodice to the skirt along the waist seam, keeping the bodice lining free. Tuck all raw edges inside the bodice, pressing the seam allowances upwards.

29 Slip stitch (see page 62) the lining of the bodice to the waistline, then bias bind (see page 54) the armholes and neck edge, but rather than topstitching to finish, slip stitch, again by hand.

30 At the top edge of the upper bodice it will be necessary to make a worked loop (see page 63), as a rouleau loop will be too clumsy on the delicate, sheer fabric.

Attach your choice of buttons and a floral corsage at the waist (see page 76) to finish the dress.

Celeste

Drift down
the aisle in a
waft of chiffon
that parts to
reveal the delicate
sparkle of beaded
silk, then simply
remove the elegant
train when you take
to the dance floor for
the rest of the night.

Celeste

This dress contains a secret support bodice, perfect for taming curves and supporting the weight of heavy beaded fabric in this strapless style. It has been designed to be very close fitting over the bust then flowing in layers of diaphanous chiffon from an Empire waistline – perfect also for hiding a bit of a tummy. Or drop the seam to your natural waistline if you prefer, choosing the line that is most flattering for you.

Making the Foundation Bodice

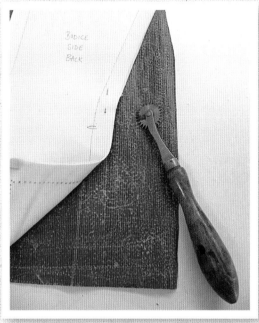

1a

1b

1 Use your personalized bodice pattern to create the foundation bodice. As this dress is designed to be fastened under the left arm with an invisible zip, there is no need to have a seam at the Centre Back (CB). Prepare the pattern by slicing off the CB seam allowance, and add a 'cut on fold' marking.

Cut all the pattern pieces in both foundation fabric (such as a sturdy cotton canvas) and lining fabric. Trace seam lines and notches onto the foundation layer of all the bodice foundation pieces, with either a tracing wheel and carbon paper (**1a**) or with an invisible/vanishing pen before mounting the foundation fabric to the lining (**1b**). (See Step 4, page 94.)

2 Pin and stitch the mounted bodice foundation panels together, leaving the side seams open (bearing in mind that for this foundation layer the lining is the 'right side'). Press the seams open, clipping curves where necessary (see page 50 for curved seams) (**2a** & **2b**).

3 Attach suitable boning (I suggest spiral boning – see page 68) to all the seams, then sew the right-hand side seam and attach boning as before. (Remember that the lining faces in to the body, as shown.)

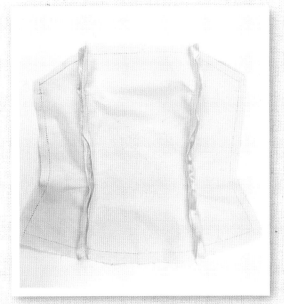

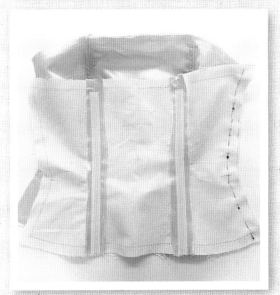

3

4

4 Attach hook-and-eye tape to fasten the bodice foundation opening. The tape I used has a built-in lapped edge so may not look the same as the tape you use, but the principles are the same. Lay the edge of the hooks flush with the finished seam line of the bodice foundation opening, tuck seam allowances in and stitch hook tape onto the bodice (using a zipper foot), being careful not to stitch over the actual hooks as this will break the needle.

5

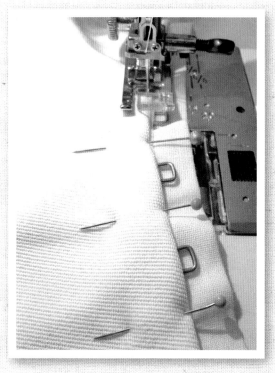

5 Repeat the process with the loop side of the tape, placing the eyes flush with the bodice edge. Make sure that once they are fastened, the hooks and eyes correspond and have not widened the opening of the foundation bodice. (For further instructions on using this product, follow the manufacturer's guidelines.)

6 Bias bind (see page 54) the bottom edge of the bodice foundation, as shown. You now have a perfectly fitting boned foundation bodice (which will be sewn into your dress as an invisible support for the heavy beading and strapless style).

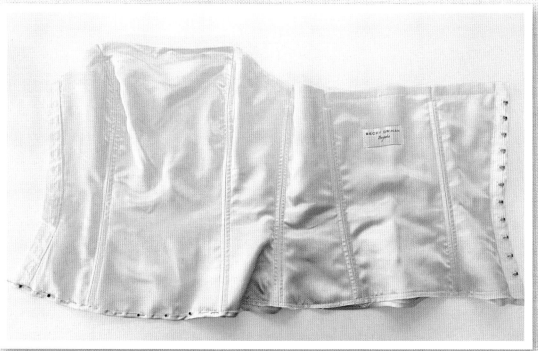

6

Drawing the Pattern

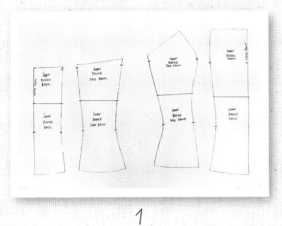

1

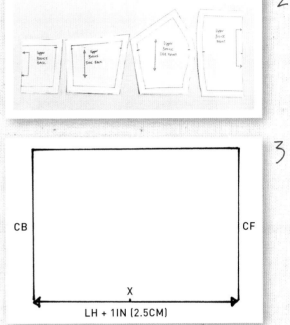

1 To make the patterns for the outer layers of your dress, use the fitted personalized bodice pattern that you toiled and created earlier. Decide where you want the waistline to sit, then mark each dress pattern piece (my seam is 3in/7.5cm above the natural waistline), measuring up along the seam line from the waist where your waist seam is to occur – the drawn line must be parallel to the waistline so the vertical seams will still match once sewn together. Label the upper and lower parts of each pattern piece, then cut along the new line. Your upper bodice pieces can now be marked up ready for using as a pattern. Put the lower half of the outer bodice panels to one side for use later.

2 As with the foundation bodice, the CB and Centre Front (CF) pattern piece will be cut on the fold. Draw around the upper bodice pieces, adding a ⅝in (1.5cm) seam allowance to all edges except the centre front and centre back. These are your final pattern pieces for the bodice.

3 To draw the skirt pattern, you need your body measurements and the lower half of the outer bodice panels you set aside earlier. Draw a rectangle – across the horizontal line it will measure 1in (2.5cm) longer than half of your Lower Hip (LH) measurement and the vertical line will be equal to your waist to LH measurement. Label the left vertical line 'CB' (Centre Back) and the right vertical line 'CF' (Centre Front), as shown. Mark halfway along the lower line of your rectangle and label the bottom point as 'X'. Take the CF and CB lower bodice panels and match them up to the vertical lines, matching the waistline on the bodice piece to the upper line of the rectangle.

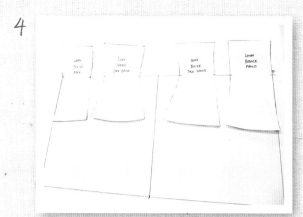

4 Place the side back and side front lower bodice panels (also matching the waistline) onto the rectangle. The bottom corners of these panels need to be ⅜–¾in (1–2cm) from that of the CF and CB panels, as shown. Once happy with the layout, stick the pattern pieces down to stop them moving.

5 Draw a line between the bottom side corner of the bodice panels (they should not be overlapping the central vertical line) and X.

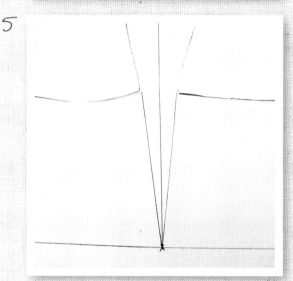

6 Extend the remaining seam lines of the bodice panels down until they converge. These will become single-ended darts. Cut out these new shapes so that you have two pieces, one for the front and one for the back. You'll need these to draw the front and back of the skirt sections. Trace the new pieces you've created (you may need to stick several pieces of paper together for the next step to cut out the full length of your skirt).

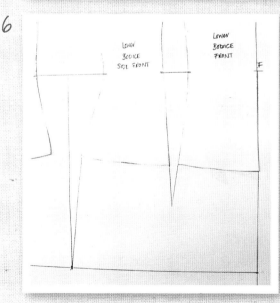

7 Extend your CF line, using your Waist to Hem (W/HEM) measurement (measuring from the natural waistline and not the new raised waistline), then extend the side seam line to equal that of the CF (you can now decide on the fullness of your skirt) before extending the existing Waist to Lower Hip (WLH) line straight from the lower hip point. You could make the skirt wider or slimmer at the hem by altering the angle of this line, but take care not to exceed the width of your fabric. Repeat this process with the back skirt. Your skirt patterns should resemble the diagram.

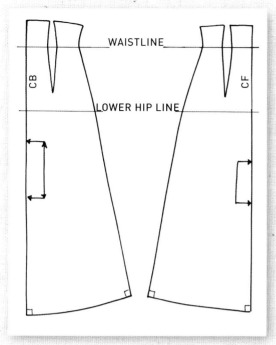

WAISTLINE

CB

CF

LOWER HIP LINE

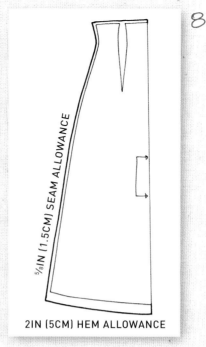

⅝IN (1.5CM) SEAM ALLOWANCE

2IN (5CM) HEM ALLOWANCE

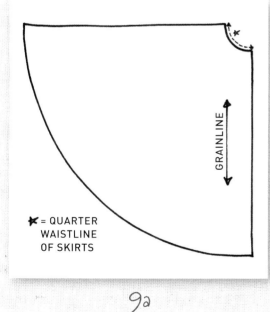

GRAINLINE

✖ = QUARTER
WAISTLINE
OF SKIRTS

9a

SELVEDGE

CENTRE BACK SEAM

CENTRE BACK SEAM

SELVEDGE

9b

9 To make the optional sheer overlay for this dress, you will need to cut a pattern for a quarter circle, the straight sides equal to the length of your other skirt panels, and the waist curve equal to quarter waist seamline (**9a**) (see page 91 for more on cutting circle skirts). Refer to the diagram as a guide for the correct shape. The optional train can be most economically cut from any sheer fabric that is the same on both sides. The shape you cut should look like diagram **9b** and can be cut as long as you like, providing it is longer than the skirts of your main dress.

8 Add ⅝in (1.5cm) seam allowance onto the side seams and top edges (bridging the gap where we've drawn darts) and add a 2in (5cm) hem allowance at the bottom edge. Cut out the skirt pattern pieces.

Making the Dress

Once you have a fitting pattern, we are ready to cut the fabrics. You should have:

- ▪ outer bodice pattern (with any toile alterations) – for foundation fabric, lining and main dress fabric
- ▪ skirt pattern, for main dress fabric and lining
- ▪ skirt overlay and train pattern, for overlay fabric that includes four bodice drapes, four skirt drapes and two panels for the train drape (the quantity of fabric you buy will depend upon the width of your fabric and the fullness of the drapes – for this dress, I used 26ft (8m) of silk chiffon at 55in (1.4m) wide.

Cut out and mark up all the pieces of your dress. Using your outer bodice pattern, you can now make a toile for your dress (see page 44). Use calico for the bodice and skirt and, if you wish to toile the drapes, use a fine fabric such as muslin. Once the toile is complete, tack it to the top edge of the foundation bodice (this will give the toile the necessary support for fitting purposes). Try the whole mock up on, make any adjustments to the toile, and transfer these alterations to your outer bodice and skirt pattern pieces.

1 Cut out and mark up all the pieces of your dress. Mount the bodice outer fabric and the lining fabric (only needed if the outer fabric is sheer) onto the corresponding foundation fabric, by hand (see page 94).

2 If you are working with beaded fabric, crush all the beads that fall within the seam allowance with small pliers (protect your eyes from fragments of glass), of all the bodice and skirt panels.

1

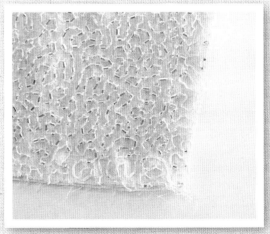

2

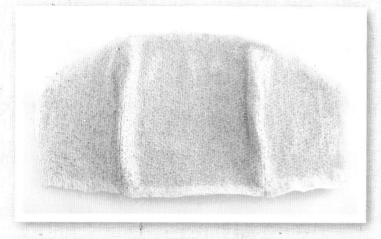

3

4

5

6

3 Pin and sew the seams of the bodice front together and repeat with the bodice back, but do not sew the side seams yet.

4 Tear or cut two strips of your overlay fabric twice the depth of your upper bodice using the full width of the fabric. Cut these in half to create four shorter rectangles. These will become your bodice drapes. Finish the long edges of the bodice draping as well as the sides of the skirt and train draping, in a manner suitable for the fabric you have chosen. Here, I used a fine satin stitch (see page 61) on the overlocker.

5 Gather one unfinished end of each piece of the bodice draping (for gathering technique, see page 80).

6 Place the bodice draping onto the right side of the bodice, lining up the raw edges at the sides, and along the top edge if desired.

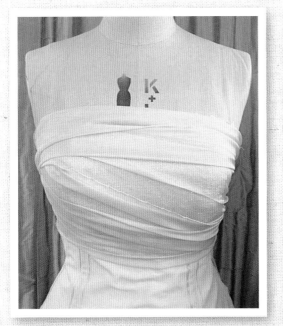

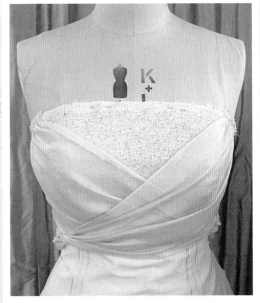

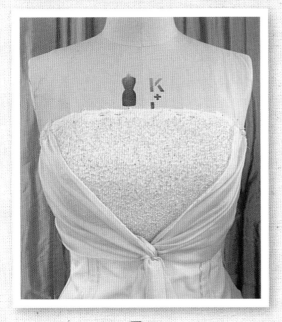

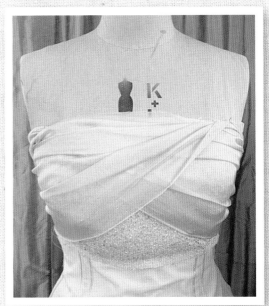

7 This next step is easiest to achieve with the bodice pinned to a dress stand. Experiment with the draping on the bodice until you find a style that best pleases you.

Pictured above are a few ideas (**7a–7d**) – I have chosen **7c** but will lose the tails of the drape into the underbust seam.

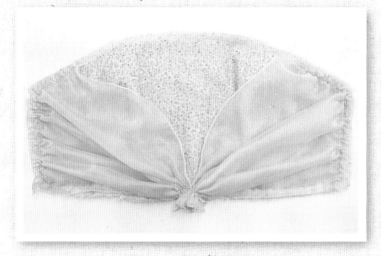

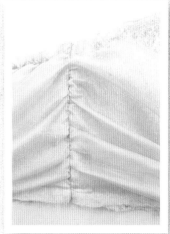

10a

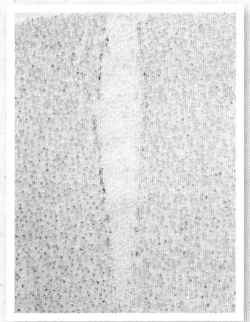

10b

8 Once happy with your draping style, tack and stitch it into place within the seam allowance, then trim off any excess fabric before repeating with the bodice back.

9 Sew the right-hand side seam together (right sides facing) and press the seam open.

10 Within the dart markings on the skirt outer, use a pair of pliers to crush the beads (this is to reduce the bulk in the finished dart) (**10a** & **10b**).

11

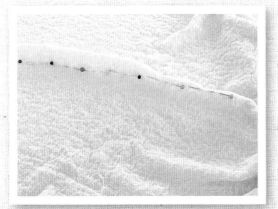

12a

12b

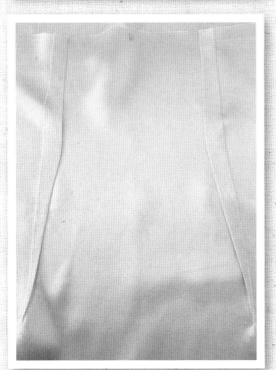

13

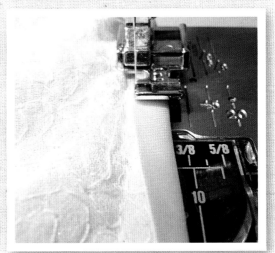

11 Pin and sew the darts in the back and front of the skirt outer.

12 Pin and sew the single-ended darts in the skirt lining (see page 65) (**12a**) then press them towards the centre (**12b**).

13 Sew the right-hand side seam of the skirt outer and skirt lining (bearing in mind that lining fabric faces right side inwards). Finish the seam allowances as appropriate. If, like me, you are using beaded fabric, then crush the beads within the seam allowance and use bias binding (see page 54) to finish. Use a zipper foot to topstitch binding, to avoid stitching over the beads.

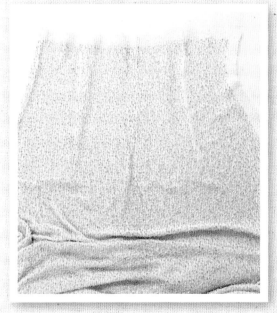

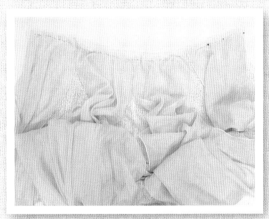

17

16

14 Sew the right-hand side of the lining together with a French seam (see page 55).

15 On both outer skirt panels on the left-hand seam, iron a bias strip of interfacing to the wrong side of the fabric, approximately 1in (2.5cm) wide, from top edge to 1in (2.5cm) below the bottom of the desired side opening in preparation for the zip.

16 This is what your skirt sections will look like from the right side of the fabric.

17 Lay out the skirt draping onto the skirt outer, lining up the raw edges of fabric at the waist seam, and pinning, then tacking them into position.

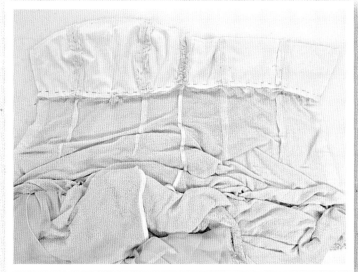

18a

18b

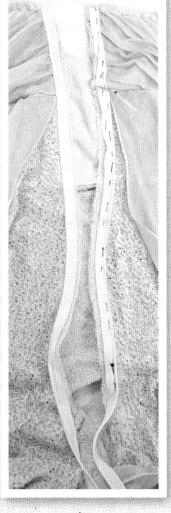

19

18 With right sides together, pin the bodice to the skirt along the waist seam, matching CF, CB and side seams (**18a**). Stitch and press the seams up towards the bodice (**18b**).

19 Trim the seam allowances along the waist seam, but stagger the lengths to graduate the bulk within the seam allowance, then insert the zip (see page 74) down the left-hand side opening of the dress.

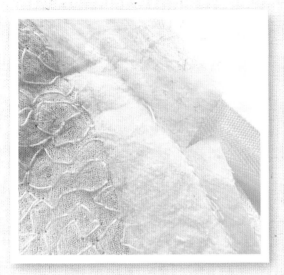

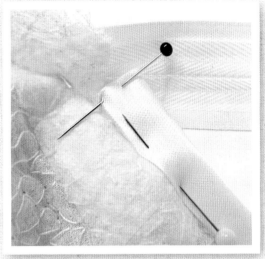

21a

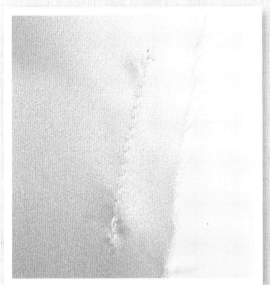

21b

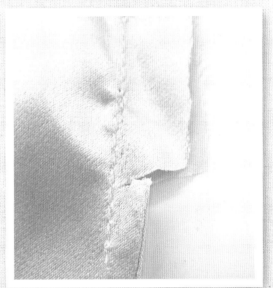

20 Stitch the side seam from the bottom of the zip to the hem, then clip into the seam allowance, level with the bottom of the zip opening, taking care not to cut the stitching (**20a**). Trim seam allowances below the zip and bias bind to finish, turning under corners of the binding (**20b**).

21 On the lining, reinforce the stitch line at the bottom of the zip opening with a couple of inches of stay stitching (**21a**). Clip into the seam allowance, level with the bottom of the zip opening, and stitch the side seam from level with clipped point to hem, finishing the seam allowance with a French seam (see page 55) (**21b**).

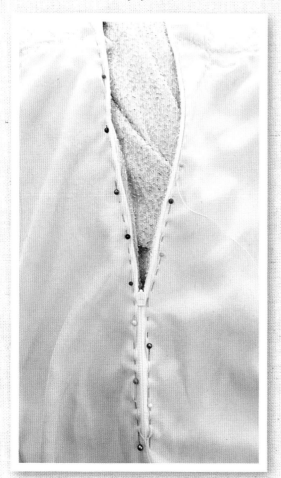

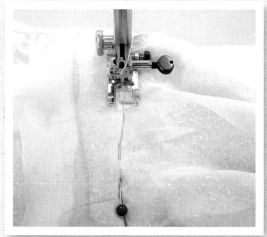

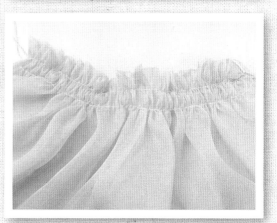

22 Slip the skirt lining inside the dress, wrong sides facing, and match up the darts, side seams and zip opening. Now tack the lining along the waist seam line, to the seam allowance. Slip stitch (see page 62) the lining around the zip inside.

23 From the right side of the bodice, 'stitch in the ditch' (see Glossary, pages 170–1) along the waist seam, through all layers of seam allowances. This is to reinforce the waist seam, and hold the lining in place.

If you are not having a detachable train, skip to Step 27.

24 For the train, sew the long edges of the train panels together with a French seam. Finish the sides and hem of your train (I have chosen an overlocked satin stitch finish). Gather the top unfinished edge of you train (see page 80), pulling the threads until your train reaches the width you desire.

27a

27b

25 Bias bind the top edge of your train and slip stitch for a neat finish. Remove the gathering threads.

26 Attach the male part of poppers (snap fasteners) and hooks alternately along the wrong side of the bias-bound edge of the train, as shown (see page 73). Sew the corresponding female part of the fastenings onto the dress along the waist seam at the centre of the back.

27 Pin your dress to the stand, then arrange your chosen decoration for under the bust – here, I have created an asymmetrical spray of floral motifs cut from an embellished lace fabric, but you can use anything from a piece of braid or a length of antique lace. There are lots of beautiful bridal trims available (see page 173 for suppliers). Pin it securely and remove the dress from the stand (**27a**). Hand sew the decoration, using a double thread and tiny stitches (**27b**).

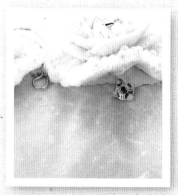

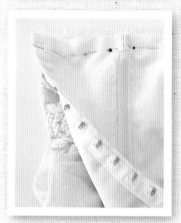

30b

29 30a

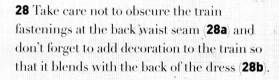

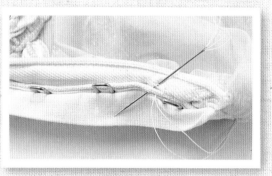

31

28 Take care not to obscure the train fastenings at the back waist seam (**28a**) and don't forget to add decoration to the train so that it blends with the back of the dress (**28b**).

29 With right sides together, pin your finished bodice foundation to your dress outer, matching the seams and keeping the top edges level.

30 Stitch the dress and foundation together along the top edge, then trim away any excess bulk from the corners of the seam allowances (**30a**). Press all layers of the seam allowance towards the lining and then understitch the seam (see page 50)

(**30b**). Trim away excess fabric from the seam, staggering the lengths to avoid creating a 'step' in the seam allowances.

31 Hand stitch the zip tape to the hook-and-eye tape from the top edge down to the waist seam as shown – this will stabilize the bodice and enclose all the rough edges.

Try your dress on and get someone to pin the level for your dress hem (see page 56 for advice on hemming). Finish the hem of each layer of the dress using the most appropriate technique. I would suggest satin stitching for the skirt drapes, bias binding and hand lockstitch for the beaded main fabric, and a double turned, topstitched hem for the lining.

Stand back and admire your finished dress... if you wish to add extra beading or sparkle, do so with moderation – it is easier to add than remove.

Florence

With antique lace
and soft crumples
of duchesse satin, this
dress is as romantic as
they come – just add your
very own Prince Charming.

Florence

This dress has a fully boned bodice and decorative but practical lacing that you can loosen or tighten throughout the day. The laced back and full train make this dress feel like a real fairytale gown, and you can really layer up those underskirts for an even more dramatic look. Add detachable cap sleeves or a lace bolero for modesty yet show-stopping appeal.

Drawing the Pattern

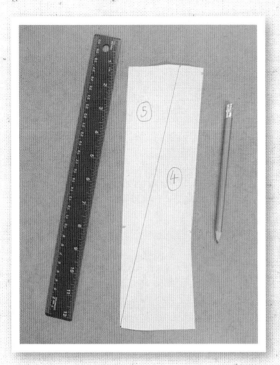

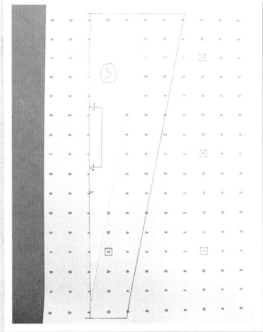

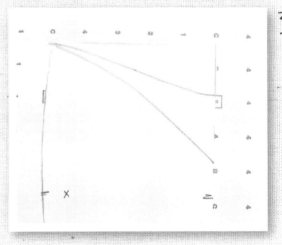

1 For this dress you can use your personalized bodice pattern with very few adjustments (see pages 40–3 on how to measure and use the patterns at the back of the book). First, take the Centre-Back (CB) pattern piece and draw a new line from the bottom CB corner to the top edge, approximately two thirds of the way from the CB line to the side-back seam line. Cut the pattern piece along this line, keeping both pieces (mark the 'wedge' as 5 and the larger piece as 4).

2 Using piece no.5, add 1½in (4cm) to the slanted edge and ⅝in (1.5cm) to the top and bottom edges – the original CB line will be cut on the fold of the fabric, so mark the pattern piece accordingly. This piece is your placket pattern.

3 Now tweak the neckline on pattern piece no.1. You may wish to leave the bodice as a straight-across neckline but for a sweetheart neckline (the one I have used), draw the upper line as shown; for a V-neck, use the lower line.

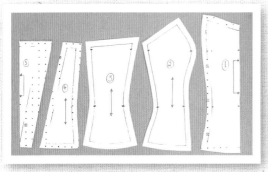

4

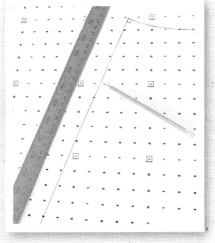

5

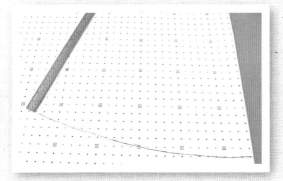

6

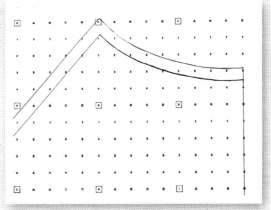

7

4 All other bodice pattern pieces can remain unaltered. Trace each piece out accurately, adding ⅝in (1.5cm) seam allowance to each edge – except the Centre-Front (CF) edge, as this will be cut on the fold of the fabric. The upper edge of your bodice can be altered further in a toile fitting.

5 For the skirt, start with the CF panel. At the top left-hand corner of a large piece of pattern paper, draw a shallow curve, equal to the length of the seam line of the lower CF bodice panel – this is the top edge of the skirt's CF panel.

Draw lines from the corners of your curve at a right angle to the curve, extending to the desired skirt hem length, as shown. (If the hem is floor level then this measurement will be waist to floor, minus the measurement of waist to the lower edge of the bodice, to equal the skirt length.)

6 Mark the same length straight down from the CF point as well. At the bottom of these two lines, draw in the curve of the skirt hem, making sure that the corners are at right angles, as shown. Mark the right-hand side edge as CF, with relevant 'cut on fold' marking. Add a seam allowance of ⅝in (1.5cm) to the top edge and side seam and a 1½in (4cm) hem allowance at the bottom edge.

7 For the skirt side front panel, repeat this process, using the side front bodice panel measurement, this time leaving a space around the pattern, allowing you to add a seam allowance to both sides of the pattern.

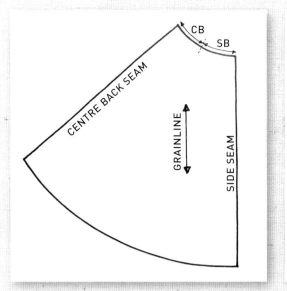

8a

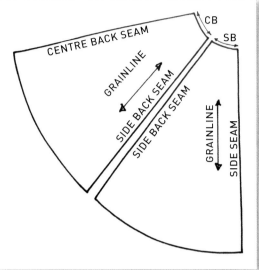

8b

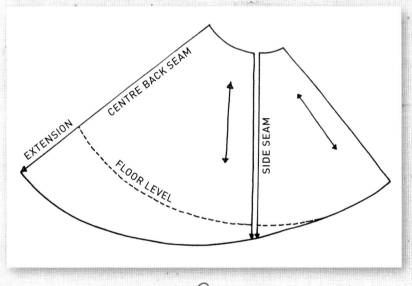

9

8 For the back skirt panel, use a combined measurement of the lower edge of the CB and side-back bodice panels to make each side of the back skirt in one large panel (**8a**). If you have a narrow fabric then use the individual back bodice measurements and make two pattern pieces, thus creating four panels for the skirt back (**8b**).

9 To draw a skirt with a train, using a fresh sheet of pattern paper, extend the CB line to the length you desire and draw a large curve from the CB hem point (making sure that this point starts at a right angle). Continue the train round so that it tapers just into the skirt's side front panel.

Making the toile

Once you have all your pattern pieces, cut and sew together a toile (using calico) for the skirt panels (see page 44). You will ideally need to try it on over whatever underskirts you are going to wear so have these ready and made if you are doing your own (see page 78) before fitting the toile.

Instead of making a toile using the adjusted bodice pattern for this particular dress – it won't meet at the centre back due to the adjustments we have made for the lacing – use the personalized bodice pattern toile you made earlier. Match up the seams and sew the skirts to the bodice, make any necessary alterations (especially to the neckline), and adjust the patterns accordingly.

Making the Dress

We can now begin to make your dress. You should have:

- adjusted bodice pattern pieces, including placket, in main dress fabric, interlining and lining fabric
- a skirt pattern (in 3 or 4 pattern pieces, to create 5 or 7 panels), in main dress fabric, lining fabric and sheer overlay fabric
- approximately 1¾yd (1.5m) of fabric for skirt draping – in sheer overlay fabric
- lace fabric for the bodice, and lace trim for skirt and bodice edges
- about 30in (76cm) extra fabric for bodice waist draping – we will cut a pattern for this later.

Cutting fabric

Cut each of the bodice pattern pieces in outer fabric, interlining (I used a strong cotton canvas) and lining fabric (for tips on how to do this, see page 47). Lay the pattern pieces onto the folded fabric, with the CF bodice on the folded edge.

Cut the skirt panels in the outer fabric, lining and overlay. Cut the CF panel on the fold of the fabric, then, for each other panel, cut two of each pattern piece, but cutting each piece on single layer fabric, flipping the pattern over after cutting the first panel, ensuring you have mirror image pairs (not two panels the same).

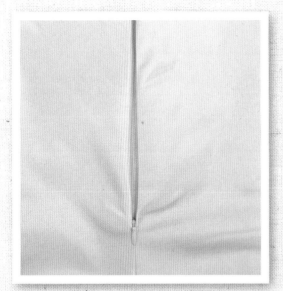

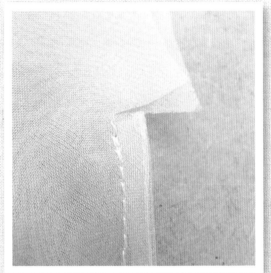

2

Sheer overlay

1 The main skirt will be fastened with an invisible zip, and the lining hand sewn to the back of the zip (we'll come to this later), but the sheer overlay needs to flow freely over the top, so we will make a delicate placket closure for this layer (this is called a continuous placket on a seam). For this, cut a strip of the overlay fabric 2in (5cm) wide and 24in (61cm) long on the straight grain. Press the strip in half down its full length and then fold one edge into the centre and press again.

2 Take the pair of CB skirt overlay panels and mark 12in (30cm) down from the CB along the seam line – snip into the fabric at this point to ⅝in (1.5cm), then French seam the fabric (see page 55) from this point to the skirt hem – to prevent fraying, use a tiny dab of fray stop glue on the cut fabric.

3 Draw along the placket strip with an air-erasable pen, marking where the second fold comes to on the non-folded half.

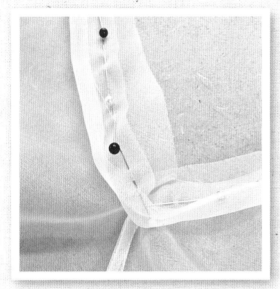

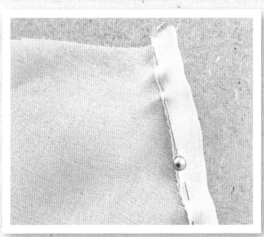

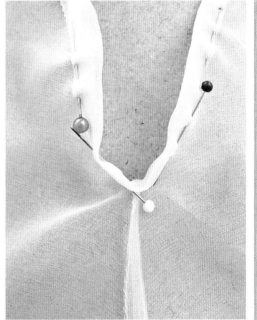

3

4 On the inside of the skirt's CB opening, lay the strip so that the drawn line matches to the seam line (at ⅝in /1.5cm from the open edge) and pin along this line. Swing the skirts round so that the CB opening lies in a straight line and continue pinning the placket across the snipped seam allowances and up the other side of the CB opening.

5 Stitch along the drawn line to attach the placket, then press the seam allowances towards the placket and trim the CB seam allowance level with the placket edge.

6 Fold the pre-pressed placket around the trimmed seam allowance and pin the edge (much as you would with a bias binding) so that the stitch line will lay on top of the previous stitching line (**6a** & **6b**). This continuous strip of fabric provides reinforcement to the delicate seam.

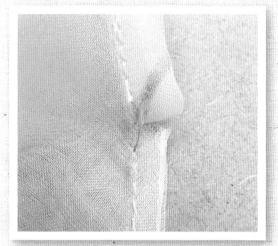

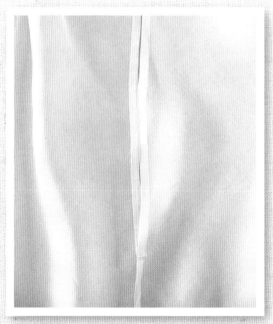

8

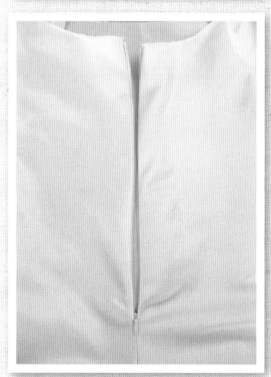

popping outwards. This placket will be fastened using tiny poppers (approximately ⅜in/1cm in diameter) – attach three pairs to the placket, spaced out evenly and not too close to the top as this will end up stitched to the bodice (see page 73).

With the placket closure finished, we can sew the side and front skirt panels of overlay to the back panel overlay, using French seams (see page 55) (**7b**).

Main skirt

8 To insert the zip into the main skirt you will need a 12in (30cm) (or longer) zip and two strips of interfacing 13 x 1in (33 x 2.5cm). Reinforce the CB edges of the skirt back panels with the interfacing (see page 29) then insert the zip (see page 74). Stitch the CB seam and press the seam allowance open. Your zip should now look as shown.

Sew the skirt fronts to the sides and the sides to the back panels, pressing the seams open.

7 Fold the skirt back panels, right sides together, pinching the placket at the bottom corner, then stitch across the corner of the placket and about 1in (2.5cm) down the existing CB seam. Pen marks indicate line to be stitched (**7a**). This stitching is to reinforce the delicate organza where it has been snipped, and to stop the placket from

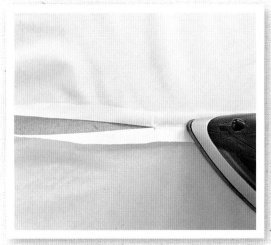

10

9 On the skirt lining, mark 12in (30cm) down from the top edge at the CB opening. Start stitching the panels together from this point down, then leave a gap of at least 20in (52cm) midway down the CB seam, then continue stitching to the hem. (This is so that we can get to the inside of the outer skirts for hemming later.) Press the entire CB seam allowance open, including where the lining will be attached to the back of the zip.

10 Get all your skirts together (lining, main and sheer overlay), layering them in the order they will be on the body – right side of lining faces legs, then skirt and overlay face right sides out. Match up the seams and the CB opening along the waistline, pinning the layers together along the seam line.

11 Stitch the skirts together at the waist, just inside the seam allowance.

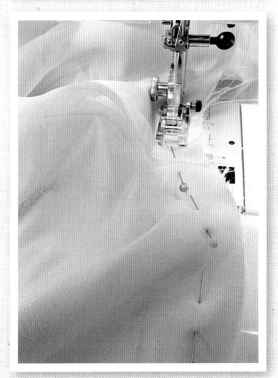

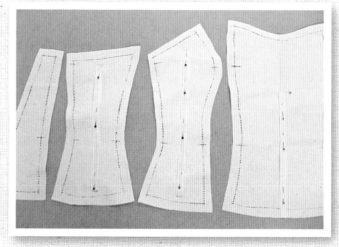

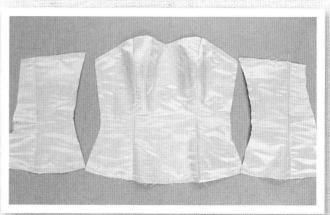

11

Making the bodice

12 For the bodice, trace the seam lines onto the interlining using carbon paper and a tracing wheel.

13 Following the straight grain, cut a piece of plastic boning (see page 67) to run lengthways down the middle of the side front and side back bodice panels and the placket. Apply plastic boning to the centre of the side front and side back interlining panels. Prepare the CF bodice interlining panel with a channel for a spiral bone (see page 68), from the bottom edge up to 1½in (4cm) below level with the fullest part of the bust.

14 Lay each panel of interlining onto the wrong side of the outer fabric and 'mount' the pieces together. Stitch either by hand or machine using a long stitch just inside the seam allowance (see page 94, Step 4).

15 Matching top and bottom edges and waist markings, pin and stitch the mounted layers of the front panels together, then the back panels together. Don't join the side seams or placket. Press the seam allowances open and clip into curves (see page 50). Prepare each seam for spiral boning by pinning and sewing a boning channel onto each one. Your front and back pieces should look like this.

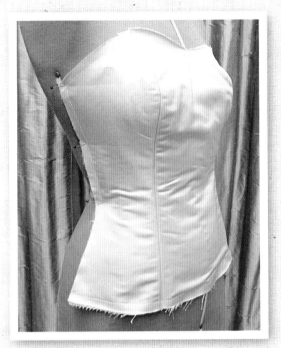

18

Bodice draping

16 Pin your bodice panels to the dress stand, take a step back and decide where you would like the draping to swathe the waistline. I have kept the bottom edge of the draping close to the bottom edge of the bodice to disguise the seam between the bodice and the skirt (see the finished dress on page 153).

17 Mark the desired drape lines onto the bodice with pins, making sure that the lines 'flow' across the seams and the CB opening. Once happy, replace pins with a row of tacking stitches (see page 62). Drape a piece of lace across the upper bust, playing with the position of the motifs, and pin the lace onto the seam allowance at the top of the bodice and down the first couple of inches (5cm) on the side seam, smoothing the lace across the upper bust area.

18 Once the fabric is smooth and pinned, the excess lace can be trimmed away from the top edge and down the sides.

19 Trim the lace off where it overlaps the upper waist drape tacking line, leaving generous 1in (2.5cm) seam allowances. At this stage the lace will probably hang off the ends of the bust points – don't worry, we'll get a smooth finish next.

20 Pin the lower edge of the lace wherever it will lie smoothly (between the boobs and in from the side seams). Here you can see how much excess lace I have below the bust point.

21 Snip carefully around the edge of a motif close to the excess lace, then slip the edge of the excess under the motif.

22 Pin carefully and catch the lace down with tiny hand stitches.

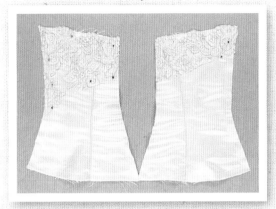

23 Repeat the draping and lace application with the back panels (as they are flatter you may be able to do this on a flat surface rather than on the dress form), as shown, then tack the lace onto all the bodice panels using large stitches within the seam allowance.

24 With the front bodice again pinned onto the dress stand, measure the area over which the bodice draping will lay.

Measure across the bodice from side to side where the upper edge of the draping is to lie (measurement 1) (**24a**). Repeat the process for the bottom edge of the draping (measurement 2) (**24b**). Measure straight across the waist (measurement 3) (**24c**). Now measure down the side seam (on.side where draping is smooth and stretched), from 1in (2.5cm) above the bottom of the lace to the lower bodice edge (measurement 4) – and from the waist to the lower edge of the bodice (measurement 5).

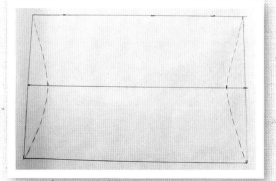

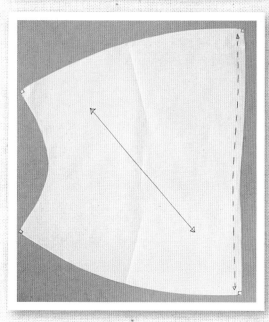

26 Your shape will resemble a squat hourglass – cut out this shape. Slice into the shape from the right-hand side, cutting to approx ⅜in (1cm) short of the opposite side, resembling 'rays' that fan out. Lay the sliced shape out onto a large sheet of paper. Splay out the 'rays' of paper, creating a more extreme curve on the left-hand side until the right-hand side is twice its original length.

27 Draw around the outer shape then remove the sliced pattern. When the drape is applied to the bodice it will flow into the side seams at a right angle to the seam, so slightly bulge the upper and lower edges out, so that the corners of your drape pattern are right angular.

The drape needs to be cut on the bias so that it can be stretched and moulded round the body. Mark the grainline onto the pattern. Down the right-hand side, mark the pattern to indicate that this edge is to be gathered with a dashed arrow extending the full length of the edge.

25 To make a pattern for your bodice drape, take a fresh sheet of paper and draw a shape using the measurements you've just taken – it will resemble a rectangle or perhaps be more of a rhomboid for you. The upper edge is equal to measurement 1, the lower edge equal to measurement 2, the vertical lines equal to measurement 4. From the lower line, measure up the distance of measurement 5 and draw another horizontal line dissecting the shape. Indent your rectangle at this point, making this line equal to the length of measurement 3.

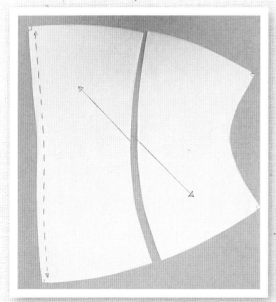

30 Pin the front drape, right side outwards with the short curve to the seam allowance of the right-hand side of the front of your bodice.

31 Gently pull the fabric across the front of the bodice and pin onto the seam allowance of the left-hand side. Gather the fullness of the fabric by hand, making small folds and pleats into the fabric, spreading the fullness evenly. Stab your pins perpendicular to the cut edge with the heads pointing outwards for easy access.

28 Trace a copy of this pattern piece in a mirror image then, finding the middle, down the length, slice the pattern in two. These two pieces can be used for the back drape.

29 Cut all three pieces from your outer fabric, laying the pattern on the right side of your fabric. Press under the top and bottom edges by ⅝in (1.5cm).

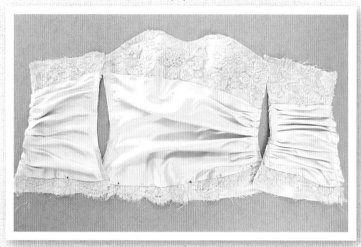

32 Due to the stretchy nature of bias cut fabric, the drape may well stretch and overhang the edge of the bodice – don't worry, just keep arranging the pleats and folds until you are happy with their appearance, Once satisfied, excess fabric can be trimmed flush with the bodice edge. Secure the gathered fabric to the bodice with machine stitching in the seam allowance.

Repeat this process using two smaller drapes for the bodice back, making sure the smooth side is once again on the right-hand side of the bodice so that the draping flows around the body.

33 Slip stitch (see page 62) the top edge of the draping but leave the bottom edge free. Using the edge trimmed from your lace fabric or a purchased lace trim, adorn the lower edge of the bodice draping. Tuck the trim beneath the drape so that an even amount pokes out following the slant. Pin the lace into position and cut the ends, leaving ⅜–¾in (1–2cm) overhanging the bodice edge at the sides. This is how your bodice should now look.

Finishing the bodice

34 With right sides together, pin the side seams together, leave the centre-back open. Double check for pins that may be hidden in the pleats of the draping. At the bottom edge, tuck one piece of lace trim back on itself and the other into the seam (so that once the seam is sewn the lace can be overlapped, making a beautiful, continuous flow around the hips).

35 Stitch the side seams, then press the seam allowance open from the inside using the tip of the iron down the centre of the seam so as not to crush the soft folds of the draping.

36 Make rouleau loops (see page 71) for the lacing that will fasten the back of your dress, cutting them into lengths of 2¼in (5.5cm).

Cut two lengths of lightweight cotton tape the same length as the CB opening of your bodice. Mark the tape at 1in (2.5cm) intervals for the spacing of the rouleau loops, leaving ¾in (2cm) top and bottom so that the loops are not too close to finish the edges of the bodice. Pin and stitch the rouleau onto the cotton tape, being careful to twist the loops so that, when stitching on the rouleau, the right side (i.e. without seams) faces out from the cotton tape.

37 Lay the prepared tape onto the CB opening with the loops pointing towards the bodice. Stitch the tape onto the bodice using two close rows of stitching for strength.

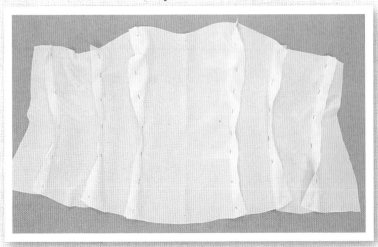

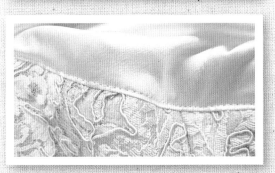

38 With right sides facing, pin and sew the bodice lining together, matching top and bottom edges and markings, leaving the centre back open (**38a**). With the right sides facing, pin the bodice outer and lining together along the top edge and down the centre back. Leave the bottom edge open (**38b**).

39

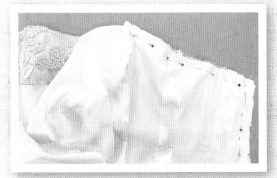

39 Stitch the bodice and lining together, following the pins and stitching perfect, sharp corners diagonally, as shown on page 51. Trim away any excess fabric at the corners then turn the bodice the right way out and press the lining towards the seam allowances. Pin the lining to the seam allowances, ready for under stitching (see page 50).

40a

40 Under stitch the centre back openings and the top edge of the bodice (**40a**) then press the finished bodice edges flat (**40b**).

40b

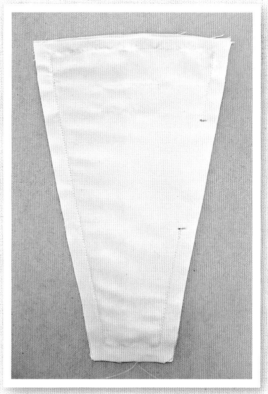

41

41 To make the optional bodice placket that
will sit underneath the laced back panel,
lay the prepared, boned and interlined
outer fabric panel, right sides facing with its
corresponding lining. (If you wish to add a
personalized label then add it to the lining
panel before stitching the placket together).
Pin the placket outer and lining together
and stitch along the seam line, stitching
across corners by a couple of stitches to
achieve sharp corners (see page 51). Leave a
gap of approximately 3in (7.5cm) down one
side so that you can turn the placket the
right way out.

42 Trim the corners and turn the placket the
right way out. Press firmly then slip stitch
(see page 62) the gap closed. Your placket
should now look like this.

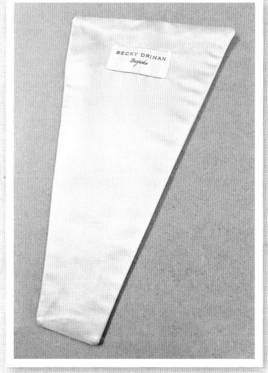

42

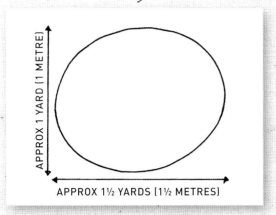

APPROX 1 YARD (1 METRE)

APPROX 1½ YARDS (1½ METRES)

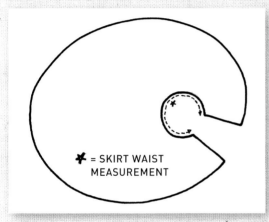

✱ = SKIRT WAIST MEASUREMENT

Skirt draping

43 To make the skirt drape, take a fresh sheet of pattern paper and draw a large oval or egg shape approximately 40 x 60in (1.5 x 1m). Make sure that the shape you draw will fit onto the width of your sheer overlay fabric.

44 Draw a wedge shape jutting into the oval at one of the narrower ends, with a roughly circular shape joined towards the sharper end of the wedge (approximately a third of the way into the oval) – the circumference of the circular shape should equal the waist measurement of your skirts (the finished shape within the original oval should resemble an oversized keyhole).

45 Cut the shape in a lightweight toile fabric then, with your skirts on the dress stand, arrange the draping over the skirts (with the break sitting on the front of the left hip), so that the angle of the draping echoes the angled lines of the bodice.

46 Pin the draping waistline to the skirts' waistline all the way around the waist, ignoring the fact that the centre back opening doesn't line up with the break in the drape. Make any alterations to the drape's shape or fullness and, using tailor's chalk, mark the point at which the drape crosses the zip and the side seams onto the toile. When you are happy with the drape, remove it from the stand, make any alterations to your pattern and cut the shape from your sheer overlay fabric, being sure to transfer all the markings using tailor's chalk or a fade-away marker.

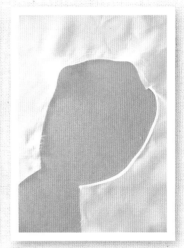

49

50

47 Stay stitch the inner edge, and finish the outer edge in the same manner as you wish to hem your overskirt (see page 59 for lace-bordered hems).

48 Snip into the seam allowance at the zip point (centre-back) and bias bind (see page 54) the top edge of the drape from the zip point, around the left hip to the gap, with a narrow binding in the same fabric.

49 Gather the edges of the wedge (see page 80) – pulling the threads as tight as they will go. Then neaten off the raw end of the left-hand end with another short length of bias binding – leave the right-hand end unfinished.

50 Again, arrange the drape over the skirts on the stand, and pin and tack the skirts together at the waist – angle the unfinished gathered edge so that the raw edges are flush with the raw edge of the skirt waistline, leaving the bias-bound section hanging free.

Joining skirt to bodice

51 Keeping the bodice lining out of the way, pin the bodice to the skirts, matching CB and seams, still leaving the bound section of the skirt drape free.

52 Stitch along the seam line, taking care not to catch the bodice lining or lace at its bottom edge into the seam. Press seam allowances up towards the bodice.

53 Trim away excess fabric from the seam allowances, staggering the layers so as not to create a sharp 'step' in layers of fabric.

54 Bring the bodice lining over the top of the trimmed layers of seam allowance and, tucking the seam allowance up, pin the bodice lining to the skirt lining, as shown, then slip stitch along the seam (see page 62).

55

55 With the dress once again on the stand, bring the loose end of the skirt drape round to the front and tuck the end under the lace trim on the bodice, as shown. Sew hooks onto the drape and eyes onto the bodice to fasten (see page 73).

56 To attach the placket we will use poppers again – this way the placket can be removed if preferred. Try the bodice on to mark the placement then, using small hand stitches, sew three 'female' popper pieces to the inside of each side of the bodice's CB opening and their corresponding 'male' parts to the edge of the right side of the placket.

57

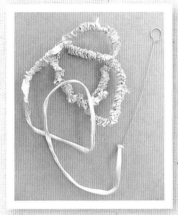

58

59

Lacing

You can use a purchased ribbon, a long length of rouleau, or flat 'tagliatelli' lacing (which we have used here). For any of these, you will need approximately 13ft (4m) of lacing, which allows for a decorative bow.

57 For the lacing used in this design, cut a 13ft (4m) long and 1½in (3.5cm) wide bias strip of fabric – you will need to join several pieces together to get this length. Press the seam allowance of any joins open then pin the strips, right sides facing and stitch ⅜in (1cm) from the folded edge.

58 Use a rouleau hook to pull the tube right-way out.

59 Press the tube of fabric flat, with the stitching line along the folded edge. Turn in the ends and slip stitch by hand (see page 62).

Useful Tip

Lace your bodice from top to bottom. Find the centre point of your lacing before starting so that you'll have an even bow at the end.

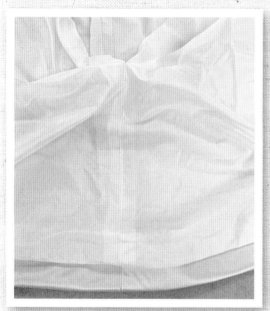

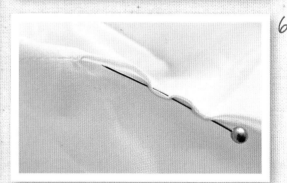

60 Try your dress on for its final fitting! With your sewing buddy's help, hitch the organza overlay up and out of the way in order to concentrate on the main skirt fabric and the dress hem. Pin your hem line as described on page 56. Lay the dress on your working surface, and tack along the actual finished hemline. Attach the horsehair braid to the hem of the dress (see page 60).

61 Now to use that hole we left in the skirt's lining seam. Lay the skirts with the hole in the lining facing you. Pull the outer skirt through the hole and, with right sides facing, pin the lining to the outer, staggering the hem allowances (as described on page 60). Pin the entire circumference of the hems through this hole.

62 Stitch, trim and press the hem, as described on page 60, then feed all of the skirt back through the hole in the lining so that the skirts are the right way out.

63 Pin and stitch the hole in the skirt lining closed by pinching the very edge of the pressed seam allowances and sewing right along the folded edge, catching the layers together.

Finishing touches

You may choose to add further detail to your dress – perhaps a corsage or two on the bodice or at the waist? Make your own in matching or a contrasting-colour fabric (see page 76), or purchase ready-made fabric flowers from a haberdashery store. You could add a little sparkle with beading, sequins or crystals (see page 64). Take a step back from your dress and see what it needs, if anything.

I have sewn seed pearls, beads and clear sequins into the lace detail at the bust of this dress to give it added texture and lustre. A couple of corsages to the hip emphasize the hitching in the organza overskirts.

Cap Sleeves

If you feel self-conscious in a strapless gown, or the place of your ceremony requires you to cover your shoulders but you don't want the full cover-up of a shrug, these little cap sleeves will be perfect. Then for an evening look, you could whip them off and dance the night away!

Measuring

To calculate the length for your sleeves, wearing the finished bodice, measure the distance from the top of the bodice from the back to front over shoulder – this is the length of your finished cap sleeve. The pieces of fabric to make the sleeves need to be longer than the measurement – by how much is up to you – the more you add, the fuller and puffier the cap will be.

For a delicate, slightly puffed effect, add approximately 3in (7.5cm) to your measurement plus ⅝in (1.5cm) at each end for the seam allowance. The next

measurement will determine how far down your arm the sleeve will fall. For the same effect as shown, measure 4–6in (10–15cm), depending upon your size (again, adding ⅝in/1.5cm seam allowance). Now draw a rectangle with your new measurements.

1

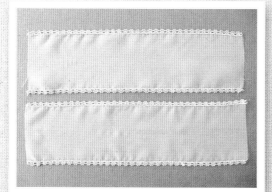

Making the cap sleeves

1 Cut two sleeves from your chosen fabric – something gauzy like chiffon, organza or tulle would be really pretty, but a lovely effect could be achieved using a lightweight satin or crisp dupion. Finish the long edges of your sleeve either by hemming or by trimming with lace or a braid (see page 56 for hemming options).

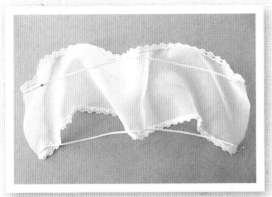

2 Cut four pieces of narrow elastic – these should be shorter than the rectangles by at least 4in (10cm), but try the length on yourself to see what feels comfortable (allow a ⅝in/1.5cm seam allowance at each end). Pin the elastic onto the wrong side of the long edges of the cap sleeves, at each end and in the centre.

3 Stitch the elastic on the cap sleeves with the sewing machine, stretching the elastic taught from front and back as you sew, so that it fits the fabric. Use a zigzag to attach the elastic (you may choose to use invisible thread).

4 Gather the ends of the cap sleeves to the desired size (see page 80) – I gathered mine to 2½in (6cm) (**4a**) – then bias bind the raw gathered edge (**4b**).

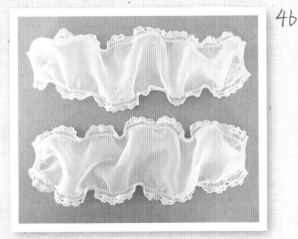

You can either stitch your cap sleeves onto the bodice by hand or make them detachable by stitching poppers or hooks and eyes (see page 73) onto the inside edge of the bodice and the outside of the bound sleeve edge.

Antique Lace Bolero

This delicate, unlined lace shrug is designed to sit snugly around the shoulders and not to be fastened at the front. It has been made in a hand-antiqued lace, so complements the lace detail of 'Florence'. With the right choice of fabric, however, it would look beautiful with any of the dresses in this book.

Drawing the Pattern

When working with lace, it is essential to cut a paper pattern piece to represent each piece of your finished garment so that you can lay each piece out individually and not rely on cutting two layers of fabric at a time. This way, you can get the most out of expensive materials and have control over the placement of the motifs within the design of the lace.

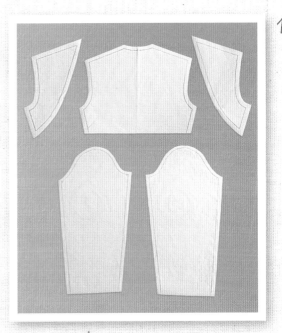

1 Select your pattern at the back of the book according to your Bust Back (BB) measurement. Cut a left and right sleeve, left and right front and a complete back panel from the provided patterns. Add ⅝in (1.5cm) seam allowance to all edges except the straight hem of the sleeves and the straight hem of the bolero back (these will be placed directly onto the lace border).

2 The sleeves of this bolero can easily be adjusted to any length you desire. Measure from your shoulder down your arm to where you'd like the hem to fall, and then transfer this measurement to your pattern. Now draw a straight line across the sleeve pattern, making sure that under arm seams are equal.

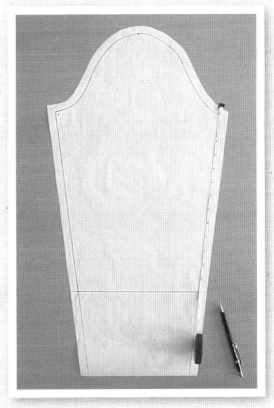

Now's the time to make a toile for your bolero. Sew all the seams, leaving the seam allowances and hems unfinished. Fit your bolero toile and transfer any adjustments to the pattern, using the instructions on page 44 as a general guide.

This is also the time to antique the lace if you are doing this, as the entire piece needs to be treated before cutting (see page 30).

Making the Bolero

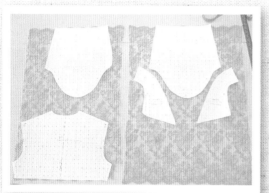

1a

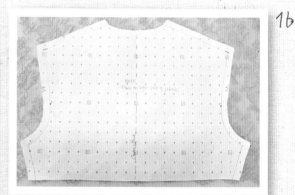

1b

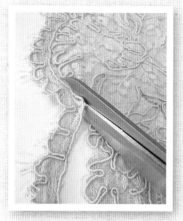

2

3

4a

1 Once you are happy with the fit, lay the pattern pieces onto the lace, taking care to keep on the straight grain (**1a**). Pay attention to the placement of motifs. Lay the straight edges of the sleeve hems and the bolero back hem onto the border of the lace (**1b**). Pin all pieces down. Cut out the fabric, taking care not to make any unnecessary snips into the border of the lace – you need this to be as complete as possible.

2 Trim the lace border from the remaining fabric, as shown – you need enough to go around the edge of your bolero front and

neck. Using an appropriate fabric marker (test markings on a spare scrap of lace to see what works – it can be different for each type of lace), transfer your markings from the pattern onto the wrong side of fabric pieces. With right sides together, lay the front and back panels facing each other, then pin and stitch the side seams and shoulder seams.

3 Make bias binding (see page 54) for the side and shoulder seams in a soft fabric that will be comfortable next to the skin – I have used a silk chiffon so that it blends with the lace fabric.

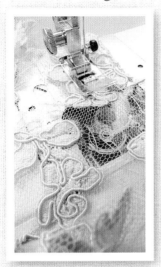

4 Neaten the end of the binding at the scalloped hem edge of the seam by tucking all the ends in (**4a** & **4b**). Stitch the binding into place and press the seam allowance to one side.

5 For the sleeves, gather stitch (see page 80) between the large dots marked on the pattern, around the top of each sleeve head, sewing at ⅜in (1cm) and ¾in (2cm) using a long stitch and no backstitch, leaving the threads long. Put the stitch length back to regular length and, with right sides together, pin and stitch the under arm seam down the length of the sleeves. Finish the seam allowances, using bias binding, as with the side and shoulder seams, and press.

6 Turn the sleeves the right way out, and the bolero inside out. Slide each sleeve into a bolero armhole so that right sides are facing one another. Match each bolero side seam to each sleeve's under arm seam, shoulder points to shoulder seams and all notches and markings in between.

Pin each sleeve's under arm curve – the fabric should lay flat with no gathers in this section. At this stage, the sleeve will be too big for the armhole, so, pulling gently on the gathering threads, ease the excess fabric of the sleeve head and distribute gathers evenly, taking care not to create pleats. Pin and stitch.

Useful Tip

By putting pins in perpendicular to the raw edge and pinning from the sleeve side of a seam, you can sew straight over any pins and control the fullness of the gathers as you sew.

7

8a

8b

9

7 As with the side and shoulder seams, use bias binding to finish the arm hole seam.

8 Press the bound seam allowance towards the sleeve (**8a**). Your finished sleeve heads will look like this (**8b**).

9 Now that we have an entire garment, it is time to apply the border lace to the bolero neck and front. Starting in the middle of your trim, match up the centre of a scallop motif to the centre back neck of your bolero, as shown.

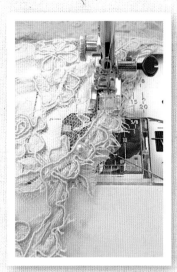

10 Place the trim so that the outer finished edge is flush with the raw edges of the bolero neck and front (**10a**), then pin the border trim all the way around the raw edges of the bolero (**10b**), overlapping the ends so that the scallop edge is continuous.

11 The lace border can be attached by hand or by using a short zigzag stitch on your sewing machine with invisible thread, as shown. (This fine synthetic thread is virtually impossible to see once sewn. Use it as you would any other sewing thread; just be sure to test it out on scraps of spare fabric to check the effect, and adjust machine tensions if necessary.) This may require two rows of zigzag stitching to secure.

12 Trim away excess fabric behind the edge of the border lace.

You can now add beading, sequins or other embellishment to your finished bolero (see page 64).

12

Useful Tip

Before stitching the border lace onto the bolero, test the stitch on scraps of lace until you are entirely happy. If using a machine, ensure you have the correct width to securely attach the lace border, and be certain that the stitch is forming correctly. Invisible thread can do funny things to the tension of your sewing machine, and unpicking it is no fun at all!

Choosing & Making a Veil

Donning a veil can be a very emotional experience and, as someone who's seen plenty of composed ladies try one on for the first time, it is often the moment when the tears arrive. Suddenly, the wedding all becomes very real and exciting!

Single Layer

Chapel Length

Birdcage

Useful Tip

Keep your veil separate from your hair ornaments. This way you can detach it without ruining your hair do.

As with all things in the glorious world of weddings, there are so many little decisions that you need to make when choosing a veil: length, fullness, materials, embellishments, number of tiers, over the face or not, attached by comb, tiara, circlet? Have a look at your wedding dress (or a drawing if you are yet to make it) and play with different lengths and styles to see what works best for you.

Measuring

Before measuring yourself for a veil you need to have decided where it is to be attached into your hair. The options include:

- from the front of the head, for example, in a tiara or Alice band
- from the crown, in an up-do
- from the nape of the neck, for example, tucked beneath a bun (this type looks best left to hang down the back rather than being pulled forward to cover your face).

If your veil is to be worn covering your face, measure from where you'd like it to start (this could be anywhere between your hips and your shoulders) to the point at which it will be attached into your hair. Consider the detailing on the bodice of your dress, if you will be carrying a bouquet, and who will lift your veil when you reach the point of saying your vows – these could all affect your decision. Make note of this measurement. Next, measure from the attaching point to where it will end. The only rule is that the back should be longer than the front (unless you're wearing a birdcage veil – see page 166).

Draw a scale diagram of your veil first to check that the measurements you have in mind will work. You will be restricted by the width of the tulle that you can buy, so check the width and make sure not to expect your finished veil to be any wider than this.

Fabrics

Choose a fine, wide, veiling tulle that is a good match with the style and colour of your wedding dress. Both silk and nylon tulle are readily available in specialist bridal fabric shops, although there is a vast difference in price. Nylon tulle has a more even texture and is far more affordable. If you are considering a long veil with several tiers and lots of volume, you will find nylon tulle far more suitable than silk.

You'd be forgiven for thinking that all tulles are breathable, but if you are considering wearing your veil over your face, silk will be more comfortable and less humid than nylon. Make sure you try the tulle over both your dress fabrics and your face before making a purchase.

Useful Tip

Lay a piece of dark-coloured fabric down before working on your tulle – it will be easier to see what you are doing. Pin the tulle to the fabric underneath, up to 4in (10cm) from the cutting line. This will help prevent layers from separating and bouncing through the blades of your scissors.

Making a Decorative Base

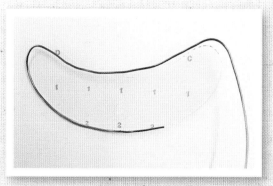
1a

1b

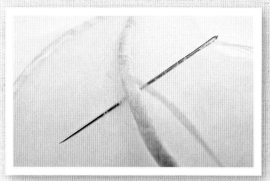
2a

2b

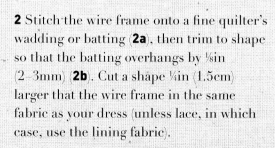
3

1 Draw your desired shape on which to model your decorative veil base then, using a soft, pliable wire, follow the outline of the pattern, going round twice and overlapping the ends by 2in (5cm) (**1a**). Bind the wire with lightweight surgical or floristry tape (**1b**) and then bend the wire shape to fit the curve of your head.

2 Stitch the wire frame onto a fine quilter's wadding or batting (**2a**), then trim to shape so that the batting overhangs by ⅛in (2–3mm) (**2b**). Cut a shape ¼in (1.5cm) larger that the wire frame in the same fabric as your dress (unless lace, in which case, use the lining fabric).

3 With the wadding facing the wrong side of the fabric, and the smooth, finished side facing your hair, wrap the seam allowance round onto the reverse, snipping where necessary to accommodate for curves. Stick the seam allowance down with small dabs of flexible glue or a hot glue gun.

4

5

PREPARING A COMB

Using a long thin strip of tulle that is approx 1in (2.5cm) wide to wrap round the base of the comb, go between each prong along the entire length of the comb. Stitch or glue the ends in place to stop this unravelling (**A**). For longer veils, the comb will be placed in your hair with the teeth facing the back of your head. For birdcage veils, the teeth face towards your face. With this in mind, stitch the veil onto the tulle of the comb using invisible thread, doubled (**B**). The comb can be decorated, or attached to a decorative base.

4 Use decorative motifs, pieces of lace, beads sequins and anything else you like to decorate your base (I have used leaf motifs to match the detail on 'Celeste', page 106). Start round the edges of the base, working your way towards the centre.

5 Now is the time to add a little extra sparkle to your headpiece using gemstone glue and tweezers.

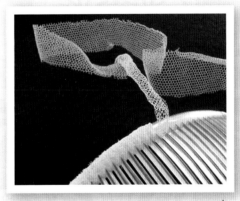

A

B

And here you have your finished veil base!

 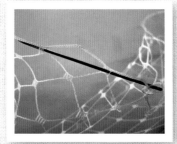 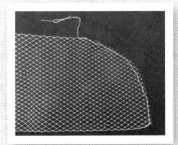

2c

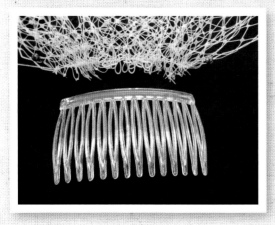

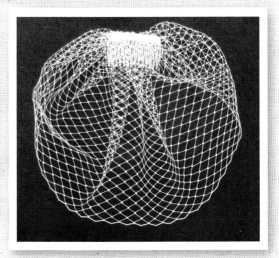

3

Birdcage Veil

For this veil, the best effect will be achieved with a stiff hat veiling – it has a large open structure and often comes in 9in (23cm) and 18in (46cm) widths. Eighteen inches will cover the entire face, ending between your jaw and your collarbones, whereas nine inches will cover your eyes and possibly lips, depending on where it is attached into your hair.

1 Measure round the circumference of your head – this is the length of net you will need. The depth of the netting you use will determine the finished veil's coverage. Fold the netting in half, trim one corner of the cut edges into a curve, then unfold.

2 Gather round the entire long curved edge of the net – stab your needle through the tight weave of the net rather than through the holes when gathering, as it will give you more control to achieve even gathers (**2a** & **2b**). Pull the threads and gather up the net to fit the comb it will be attached to (**2c**).

3 Prepare a comb (see page 165), then hand sew the veiling onto it with the teeth of comb and veiling pointing in same direction, as shown. Now you can add decoration to your veil – this could be a fabulous opportunity to add a piece of vintage jewellery or a corsage (see page 76) into your outfit.

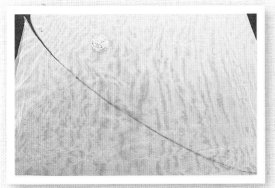

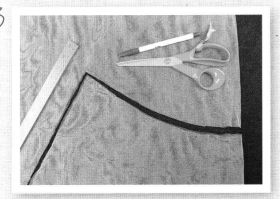

Useful Tip

Discuss your preference for a veil with your hairstylist. Unless you are prepared to backcomb your hair, you will probably need some of your hair to be 'up' in order to attach a veil.

Single-Layer Veil

1 Measure from the protruding bone at the back of your head to the desired length of your veil. Add 4in (10cm) to this length – this is how much tulle you'll need. Fold the tulle in half across the width, keeping the full length of tulle. Across the bottom, starting from the folded corner, draw a curve sweeping up towards the long sides of the folded tulle. An invisible or disappearing pen is the easiest, most accurate method of marking the tulle.

2 Draw a curve at the top end of your tulle – starting 4in (10cm) down from the top at the folded side, swing across towards the top edge. The point at which the line meets the top edge depends on the desired fullness at the top of your veil. I wanted to achieve a flared veil so I only drew the line to one third of the full width of the tulle. Connect the top and bottom curves with a straight line.

3 Cut the tulle along the marked lines using long smooth cuts with your scissors, as shown. Apply decoration and edging as you desire then gather the top edge of your veil to fit the size of the comb you are using. Attach the veil to your comb, as described on page 165.

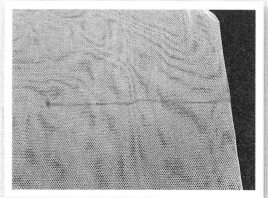

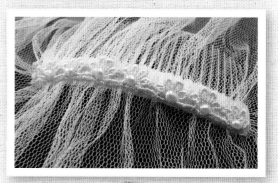

Chapel-Length Veil with Blusher

1 Measure from the desired hem of veil to crown and then from crown to front hem. Add these two measurements together to get the full length of the veil. This is how much tulle you will need. Fold the tulle into quarters, then draw a curve across the corner opposite the folds, as shown. Once opened out, the tulle will make a large oval shape. Unfold the tulle so that it is only folded once from side to side.

2 Mark the 'crown' point onto the folded edge of the veil (do this using the crown to front hem measurement), and draw a line at a right angle to the folded edge, marking the area of tulle to be gathered into the comb.

The larger the amount of tulle gathered into the comb, the puffier the finished effect.

3 Finish the edge as you wish, then gather the veil and hand sew to a prepared comb.

4 As this veil is intended to be worn both covering the face and then arranged back over the shoulders, you may wish to decorate the comb. If you are wearing a tiara, this may not be necessary as long as the veil is tucked right in behind the tiara. To add decoration to the comb, use beads, crystals, and pearls, and either hand stitch securely or use a fast-drying flexible glue or hot glue gun.

Finishing Touches

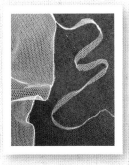

A

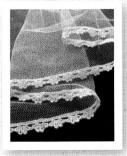

B

C

D

To finish the edges of your veil there are several choices: unfinished, corded, lace or ribbon trimmed, satin stitched or with beaded drops. Consider the density of the trim, where the finished edge will cut across your body, and how this may affect the look of your dress beneath.

Cording

Put a very fine cord or decorative thread into the bobbin of the sewing machine (I have used crochet cotton) and an invisible thread on top. Sew the edging on using a simple straight stitch on the sewing machine, approximately ⅜in (1cm) from the cut edge. You will probably need to adjust the tensions or the feed dog settings on your sewing machine, so use the off cuts of tulle to practise until the stitch lays flat and doesn't pucker. Trim the excess fabric away to ⅛in (2mm), as shown (**A**).

Lace or ribbon trim

Pin your trim to the edge of the veil and attach, either by hand or by using straight or zigzag stitch on the sewing machine with invisible thread (**B**).

Bead or crystal decoration

Attaching the beads to the bottom edge of your veil can add a delicate sparkle and also a little weight to the hem. Sew drop beads on individually, using a fine needle and invisible thread. Try and keep stitches tiny and on the same spot to avoid puckering the tulle (**C**).

Stick-on crystals and pearls

Use a small-headed pin to apply delicate spots of gemstone glue to the tulle, then use tweezers to pick up and apply the crystals and pearls. It can be really tricky on such a gauzy fabric to keep the application of stones neat. I put my finger behind the tulle, dab on a spot of glue and attach the stone. Your finger will then remove the excess glue, which you can use for the next stone. Keep the tulle flat until the glue has completely dried (**D**).

Glossary

Antiquing Ageing a fabric to give it the look of antique cloth. This can be achieved by dying the cloth with natural dyes, such as tea or coffee.

Bagged out When all the raw edges of a seam or hem allowance are caught inside a lining, creating a really neat finish on the inside and out.

Batting Known in the UK as wadding, *see below.*

Bias The bias is an invisible line that runs across the true diagonal of a fabric's grain. Fabric cut on the bias will have a natural 'stretch' and was very popular for the slinky fitted dresses of the 1930s.

Bias binding A ready-made strip of fabric cut on the bias grain with the edges folded in to the centre. It can be used to finish hems and seam allowances and is especially useful for finishing curved edges. There are products available for you to create bias binding from your own fabrics, but most haberdashery stores sell pre-made binding in a range of colours and widths.

Bodice The top half of a dress or blouse that fits the torso.

Bolero Also called a 'shrug', this is a short jacket that fits round the shoulders and arms, but often will not meet at the centre front, so is designed to be worn unfastened.

Boning Narrow strips of a material for stiffening and supporting the fabric of a garment. Historically made from whale bone or wood, now most commonly plastic or fine steel.

Bust point The fullest, most prominent point of a women's bust. When taking a bust measurement the tape measure must be level with the bust points.

Bustle A frame or pad worn beneath a dress or skirts to add fullness and volume to a lady's silhouette round her hips and bottom.

Cap sleeves Very small sleeves that just cover the top of the shoulder.

Corsage A small bouquet of flowers usually worn at the wrist, bust or waist. Flowers may be real or handcrafted from fabric or feathers.

Crin/Horsehair braid A woven nylon trim that is used inside a garment to stiffen the hem of a skirt and add volume to underskirts.

Dart A tapered, stitched tuck of fabric used to remove excess fullness usually at the waist or bust of a garment, enabling a snug fit.

Draping The art of arranging fabric on the body or a dress stand. While it is possible to cut a pattern for draping, the very nature of it means that you work with the fabric's texture, utilising its natural qualities in the 3D form. Therefore, even when a pattern is used it may be necessary to adjust the draping once actually on the dress stand.

Dress stand Also called a mannequin or a tailor's dummy, this is the 3D model of a woman's torso that we use to fit garments.

Empire waistline A style of dress popularised in the early 19th century where the waistline is raised to directly under the bust, thus emphasising the bosom and hiding the natural waistline.

French seams A seam where the raw edges of the fabric are completely enclosed, creating a finish that is as neat from the inside as out. Especially useful for sheer and translucent fabrics.

Grain Woven fabrics consist of two sets of threads that cross at right angles to one another. Those running up and down (parallel to the selvedge) are called the warp, and those running from side to side (from selvedge to selvedge) are called the weft. The straight grain refers to the warp threads, and fabric pieces should be laid and cut according to this grainline.

Interfacing Available in both fusible and sew in, interfacing is an essential material in dress making used to add body and stability to a fabric.

Interlining A layer of fabric that is sandwiched between the outer fabric and the lining, used to support the outer fabric, adding weight, bulk or stability to a garment.

Invisible zip A lightweight zip with plastic teeth that is used to invisibly fasten a garment along a seam (usually at the centre back or down the side seam).

Lining fabric The fabric used inside a garment that faces the body. A lining is important to protect the inside seams from wear and tear and helps a garment to hang nicely, skimming the body.

Mounting Layering two fabrics together and then treating them as one, this is how interlining is most commonly used.

Overlocker (serger) A special machine with three or four threads used to finish off raw edges of a seam or hem. Due to the stitch formation, an overlocked seam is stretchy and strong; they are therefore used widely in garment manufacture.

Pattern The paper guide used as a template for cutting out the pieces of a garment, the pattern will usually indicate where it will be laid on the grain of the fabric and have markings that will provide essential information for the construction of a garment.

Placket The reinforcing layers of fabric where there is an overlap at the fastening of a garment; for example, down the front of a man's shirt.

Rouleau A fine tube of fabric with all the rough edges enclosed inside. Used for straps, fastening loops and surface decoration.

Ruching Where a fabric is decoratively gathered to draw emphasis to the shape of the body or add detail to a garment.

Ruffles Strips of gathered fabric added to garments or furnishing, adding fullness and decoration.

Scallop edge The decorative, repetitively curved edge of a lace fabric.

Seam allowance The distance between the cut edge of the fabric and the stitching/seam line. In this book the seam allowance is ⅝in (1.5cm) unless otherwise stated.

Selvedge The 'finished' woven edge of the fabric that runs the entire length of a cloth. The selvedge is always parallel to the grain line of a fabric.

Staystitch A row of plain machine stitching used to prevent a seam from stretching or to hold two or more layers of fabric together before they are stitched into a seam.

Stitch in the ditch A method of stitching a seamed layer of fabric to another beneath it. Stitching directly in the crease between the fabrics of an existing seam allows the stitches to completely disappear in the groove of the seam.

Tailor's ham A tightly stuffed cushion of fabric used to provide support when pressing curved seams or tricky shapes in a garment. Especially useful when pressing bust seams or sleeve heads.

Thread shank A hand-made 'stalk' of thread that elevates a button proud from the surface of the fabric, allowing a button to fasten through thick layers of fabric without causing it to pucker.

Tiers Gathered layers of fabric attached together in successively increasing or decreasing fullness.

Toile A mock-up of a garment made from an inexpensive cotton fabric, a toile allows the dressmaker to fit a garment and make alterations before cutting into precious or costly fabrics.

Underskirts Layers of skirt worn beneath the outer skirt to add warmth, enhance a silhouette or simply make a skirt more comfortable. Underskirts are often meant to be seen, and may have decorative lace or bound hems.

Wadding/Batting A soft, thick material used most often to pad quilts. Available in natural (cotton, bamboo) and synthetic (polyester, microfibre) fibres.

Yoke A fitted part of a garment, especially at the chest or hips, from which an unfitted, looser and often gathered part of the garment is hung.

Suppliers

Fabrics and haberdashery

WWW.BRIDALLACEANDFABRIC.CO.UK

A wide range of affordable fabrics for bridalwear and proms, including plenty of good-quality synthetic fabrics.

WWW.BROADWICKSILKS.COM

An extensive and diverse range of high-quality fabrics. Thousands of beautiful silks and laces in stock for you to visualize your dress.

WWW.DITTOFABRICS.CO.UK

High-quality, affordable dressmaking fabrics. Available in-store and online.

WWW.JAMES-HARE.COM

Wholesalers of a vast range of beautiful fashion and interior fabrics. Check online for your nearest stockist.

WWW.MACCULLOCH-WALLIS.CO.UK

A well-established shop in the heart of London stocking all manner of haberdashery, trimmings and fabrics. Top-end prices but quality to match.

Pattern making

WWW.MORPLAN.COM

A great source for all your dressmaking equipment, including scissors, pattern paper and mannequins.

Acknowledgements

GMC Publications would like to thank

Chris Gloag, and his assistant Guillaume Serve, for the brilliant fashion photography.

The beautiful Ivana from Zone Models.

Jeni Dodson for hair and make-up.

Rebecca Mothersole for styling assistance.

Photo credits: Page 8 flickr/photos/sflovestory/. *Page 9 (left)* Library of Congress, Prints & Photographs Division, Toni Frissell Collection, LC-USZC4-11913. *Page 9 (right)* © Kirsty Wigglesworth/Press Association Images

For the kind loan of the tiara worn on the front cover and on pages 11, 85 and 127-9, designed by Lisa Matthews:

THE OZONE
21-23 Church Street,
Brighton, East Sussex,
BN1 1RB
Email: info@ozoneweddings.co.uk
Telephone: +44 (0)1273 739500
www.ozoneweddings.co.uk

Author's acknowledgements

Well, if you'd told me two years ago that I would write a book I'd have thought you were mad!

Thanks to everyone at GMC for finding me and believing in me, especially Dominique for her patience and Gilda for embracing my ideas, it really has been a pleasure to work with you all.

Big thanks to my friends and family for your support. To my dear friend Dizz who spent hours deciphering my scrawled hand writing and turning it into a legible text. To Gill, for inspiring me with gorgeous fabrics all my life. To my wonderful Dad for being the business brains and asking all the right questions. To my amazing Mum, who taught me to sew, and has helped endlessly with my other work whilst I've been busy writing this book. And to my gorgeous, fabulous boyfriend Rowan, for his love and encouragement, for staying up through the night just to keep me company, for his patience with me making a huge mess in our tiny house, not to mention all the takeaway meals and glasses of wine, thank you.

And thanks to you, for reading this book. Learn lots, love sewing, and wear your dress with pride. X

Index

To request a full catalogue of GMC titles, please contact:

GMC Publications Ltd, Castle Place, 166 High Street,
Lewes, East Sussex, BN7 1XU, United Kingdom

Tel: +44 (0)1273 488005 www.gmcbooks.com